Creating a 21st Century Win-Win Economy

The Problems and the Solutions

Mark Pash, CFP

Dedicated to Rayne Mckenzie Bell, Zealand Ezra Bell and all the other grandchildren of the world.

Spread the Word!

ACKNOWLEDGEMENTS

First, I wish to thank Minerva Hoover Williams, Marketing Director of the Center for Progressive Economics for motivating me to write my second book which is a chore for a non professional writer. I would like to thank our other assistants at the Center: Barbara Eisenman, Evan Blumer, Todd Hoover and Brad Parker. Brad is the author of "Left Turn Only" which has some of our solutions included and wrote much of the prose on our site (www.cpe.us.com) which was also used for this book. I also thank Doug Kreigel, Jerry Simonoff, Professor Joseph Huber, Michael Bell, and my wife, Ruth Pash, for reviewing along with Brad, Minerva, Evan Blumer, and Alex Baer. I would also like to give special thanks to Jerry Simonoff and Gail Conway for supporting the Center at inception.

Secondly, I would like to thank all the macroeconomic authors for their contributions to the development of this philosophy of solutions. Many of their books are actually listed and recognized in the text of this book. There are several that are not, which are: "Confronting Capitalism" by Philip Kotler, "Screwed" by Tom Hartmann, "Good Capitalism-Bad Capitalism" by Baumol, Litan, & Schramm, and "Debunking Economics by Steve Keen. The latter, I encourage all macroeconomic academics read! Of course, I have used the Economist Magazine and their many articles in my research over the decades.

Lastly, I want to thank all the employees of Pash & Benson, a Comprehensive Financial firm, who have to put up with all my "out of the box" discussions and computer questions: Gary Benson, CFP, Greg Meyer, CFP, Sherry Rothstein, Heather Blades, Nanette Ovejera, Zechariah Holloman, Mark Alex Jokel, Kathy Nickols, Corin Sender, and Donna Schiller, CFP. I also want to thank my family for the same reason: Ruth, Andrea, Kim, and Michael.

Table of Contents

PREFACE

It is the year 2046.

(This part is true. It was transpired in 2016).

It has been 30 years since my grandfather wrote this book. Looking back over the last 30 years, since we won the trial of the Millennium – Big Oil vs. Children in Federal Court – "Youth vs. United States Climate Case" forced the Federal government to start the elimination of fossil fuels. By coincidence, I was one of the 21 children who were plaintiffs. At the time my grandfather was heavily involved in the monetary reform movement that allowed the funding of the transition to alternative fuels and other life changing technologies.

(This case went to trial on my grandfather's 70th birthday in 2016)

(This part is a delightful fiction.)

The winning of our landmark environmental case was just in time for the next major financial-monetary crisis (not in the U.S.) in Trump's second term (2021) causing him and his advisors to read my grandfathers book and others listed in his text. These books and websites provided the evidence for monetary reform that the "debt" money creation system of the commercial banks was inherently unsustainable to be successfully regulated and create a healthy economy.

The Trump administration pushed through complete monetary reform eliminating the creation of debt money by the banks and substantially increasing the distribution systems of newly created money. This evolutionary change allowed almost unlimited funding over the years that resulted in an 85% reduction in the use of fossil fuels. They started with loans for solar installations to the large industrial buildings, shopping centers, schools, apartment buildings, office buildings and finally the smaller single-family homes. They spread long term, low cost loans geographically reducing the chances of gouging and excess inflation on equipment and installation. The regulation mandated that everyone had to convert within 10 years from the signing of the legislation. This requirement was not a burden as the property owners rushed to install, which saved money on operations. The excess energy was sold to the power companies who were required to purchase this excess by the legislation. Elon Musk immediately put thin solar panels on his Tesla car roofs eliminating the need to charge them in most climates.

The government created money for auto loans at 1% delivered by the banks and auto companies to repurchase all non-electric, driver required cars and trucks. They started with the older models buying them for a little under "Kelly Blue Book" as the down payment on a new electric-self driving car. The government sold the purchased new cars as salvage. This one-time program was spread over 10 years to avoid any excess inflationary conditions.

All the cars were electric and self-driving just in time for my grandparent's reduced ability to drive. This automobile transition saves over 30,000 lives per year not counting the reduction in injuries and property damage. Auto insurance premiums and claims plummeted. The "car guys" developed local mini warehouses, driving tracks, and roads for their classic cars and large auto resorts for their "driving" vacations.

The only fossil fuel power that they could not completely convert to renewables were the jet engines powering our airplanes. However, we continued to increase their fuel efficiency and improve their fuel mixtures so airplanes were using 60% less fossil fuels over the last 20 years. The big container and other freighters converted back to sails and solar with oil as a much lesser fuel only when needed. We created very large blimp like cargo planes that were only fueled by solar and sail that were faster and less expensive than ships.

The oil and gas companies were converted to energy companies and still supplied the world with the non-fuel use of oil. They were substantially reduced in size but with their reserves and the deductibility of their dividends they still proved excellent investments. Even Saudi Arabia changed to an "Energy Country". The Arabian Peninsula was the perfect location for solar, wind and algae fuel production, also research and development.

We converted our unused oil and gas tankers, creating a fleet of the world's largest trash collectors. This started the cleanup of our oceans especially in the northern Pacific Rim. New technology (funded by government grants) allowed us to pulverize, incinerate and recycle this trash. This clean up allowed our oceanographers to be able to regenerate the oceans and grow more fish for human consumption.

The health industry also took these unused oil and gas tankers, along with the old fossil fuel powered cruise ships, and converted them to giant clinics and hospitals to provide health care for those regions with scarce services. The converted tankers were parked in the harbors of West Africa and traveled to remote islands. Medical students were thrilled to give service to humanity in exchange for all their schooling costs, there was no shortage of personnel. Now, quality healthcare has almost reached everyone around the world. This was based on the old Cuban strategy of educating and exporting doctors and other health care providers. Everyone of my generation expects to live past his or her 100th birthday as cancer, heart disease and diabetes have been eliminated by the explosion in medical research and technology that was more adequately funded by true monetary reform. Good health will continue to be aided by the massive expansion of the organic food industry.

The internet and robotic explosion resulted in many people not having to work in the cities thus buying small organic farms for their homes, and creating substantial competition for the giant corporate farms. These small farming operations have been totally automated for over three decades. It forced the big corporate farms and food processors to increase their quality and the increased supply kept prices down. Mortgages issued by the government's "new money" for primary residences and by the private sector's "old money" for the purchase of larger or second homes facilitated these home-farm purchases. These mortgages were delivered and serviced by the large commercial banks, local community banks, credit unions and mortgage brokers. In addition, substantial number of low cost mortgages of new money was available for all the low-income housing-apartments and energy conversions in the cities. Other real estate projects were funded with "old money" from the private sector. Again, by spreading these loans over time and location, the economy avoided any significant asset bubble-inflation.

The banking industry boomed with all the new deposits and loans they provided the public without the worry of their periodic collapses. The antitrust department had to break up a few large banks that had too much market share. These spin offs resulted in the increase of competition keeping their fees and charges at a lower level and the interest they paid their depositors at a higher level.

The food industry developed the technology to cheaply manufacture protein in terms of beef, pork, lamb and poultry that tasted great and was more nutritious and safer to eat. This significantly reduced the herds, which reduced the production of methane gas (a very large producer of carbon causing climate change). This protein product was consumed in daily meals and the actual herds were saved for specialty restaurants and holiday meals. The ranchers had to do a little adjusting to other farming but remember all their basic living, sustainable expenses were covered.

Even though our ecological system was reverting to a more normal cycle, we still had periodic fresh water shortages in the more arid areas of the globe. These shortages were easily solved by implementing the low tech, micro irrigation and conservation systems that Israel had developed almost since its creation in 1948. It is now one of their biggest exports. We now have solar powered desalination plants and a few of those big oil tankers were converted to water carriers with desalination equipment aboard for emergencies around the world.

Everyone has the opportunity to get a free education in the area of study they desire. We do not have to worry about making money to cover our survival expenses. The world governments provide the funds or actual services for health care, food, shelter, clothing, along with education. Most were still delivered by an array of competitive business organizations both for profit and nonprofit. If a country had a substantial trade surplus causing their currency to be stronger, they gave a small percentage of their currency back to other countries that had trade deficits. This process was a win-win as the recipient of the currency just continued to purchase goods and services to the countries that gave the currency and kept excess inflation at bay around the world.

Since A.I., robotics and other technologies have substantially reduced the need to work, especially in manufacturing and farming; our workweek was down to 24 hours around the world with 4 to 6 weeks of vacation and personal time. My grandfather predicted in his book the massive explosion of the leisure industries because of these developments. Therefore, I selected the performing arts as a career and my sister went into the art world. There was plenty of private and public capital for the rapid expansion of live theaters and entertainment or museum complexes around the world.

The new federal land bank created money to purchase extra land around the national parks and other regional parks to expand the areas for leisure and conservation. The government sold federal land that had never been used to reduce the money supply keeping inflation in check.

Fortunately, my sister and I were in the top 1% of wealth because of our inheritance, so we could do things that others could not afford, but the others did not care as they had a chance to work in the fields of their choice. They could make money through business and investment ownership and have plenty of leisure time to pursue the cultural and volunteer areas of their choice. Most of these goods and services are still provided by many non-government owned organizations with substantial competition keeping inflation in check. Real monetary reform eventually eliminated income and payroll taxes on 80% of the population reducing the need for large tax collection agencies. The wealthier still pay income taxes to keep inflation in check and estate taxes to encourage foundations and provide recirculation of money. The government funding of basic benefits (when used) are also taxable to the rich as ordinary income.

The lowering of the corporate tax rate on net profits was competitive with other countries tax rates. This tax rate change resulted in a significant influx of corporate headquarters to the United States. The main reason was security and our extensive repair of our infrastructure. Our massive military budget affords better protection than smaller countries. The addition of a gross profits tax on all companies, foreign and domestic, offset the decline in tax revenues from lowering the net profits tax rate.

What stopped the conversion of fossil fuels in the early 21st Century was the scarcity of money! Complete monetary reform eliminated an artificial scarcity that allowed the transition funding for businesses and individuals by loans, investments and some direct grants. It is hard to believe that my grandfather's monetary reform movement by freeing up "money", which cost nothing to produce and could release so much human capital to make the world and his grandchildren's lives even better than his.

When the industrial powers started to initiate these basic services, the concern was illegal immigration to attain these benefits. Initially, we had very strong restrictions on who received the benefits and low legal immigration until about a dozen years ago. Now most countries around the world have implemented them and it did not matter too much, where you lived. Of course, there are cultural differences especially in diet and housing. The U.S. did substantially increase legal immigration from the Philippines to take care of the aging baby boomers. The caretaker robots that existed at the time of the writing of his book were not capable of doing all the variations of this type of care.

Most people wanted to work for self-satisfaction and the extras that a salary provided. Many still wanted to get rich to obtain nicer cars, expensive homes and luxurious vacations. Human wants still provide substantial motivation for innovation, management advancement and entrepreneurship. The reduction in work time and expanded funding by the new monetary system combined with the private financial system provide enough employment for the entire five billion global work forces. The rest of the little less than four billion people were children, disabled and retirees. There are very few who do not want to put in their 24 hours to contribute to the global economy. With the global change in the economy and expansion of women's rights there is no reason for large families, so our population growth leveled off, reducing the strain on nonrenewable resources.

Because the basics of life are provided for all, environmental technology reduced the natural resources competition; country conflicts are minimal. Everyone knows that we are all interrelated and need each other. Criminal behavior was also reduced, as people no longer have to rob or sell drugs to survive. Yes, we still have conflicts and crime; it still is difficult for humans to get along. We all have more significant access to psychologists, family counselors, social workers and psychiatrists than in the past; not just for the mentally ill or specific problems but also for human psychological growth enabling us to get along better. We developed specialty residential villages for the mentally ill and the drug addicted doing away with the old mental hospitals, sanatoriums and jails. Life is still not perfectly equal, but we are going in the right direction for a more sustainable and rewarding future.

After repairing our infrastructure, the global community established and funded the international space organization that is in the process of building the first city-space station half way to the moon housing thousands of scientific researchers. This will lead to a permanent moon colony and extensive exploration of the solar system. We are preparing ourselves for the 22nd Century and beyond. My grandfather was a huge Star Trek fan, from its inception, and his dream of that type of existence is really coming true. He told me that it does not matter if anyone knew about his macroeconomic contributions to improve the world. It only matters if my sister and I know so we can contribute to the world.

INTRODUCTION

Chapter 1

THE SOLUTIONS BOOK

Microeconomics and personal finance will not be discussed here. Microeconomics is the study of businesses making sales, operations, and profits. This book is about macroeconomics which is the other branch of the economic discipline that studies the overall condition and behavior of a country's economy. The size of the macroeconomic pie is unlimited. The age of scarcity is over, because the current capacity and productivity of the private sector can grow and produce all the goods and services that everyone needs as long we use **proper resource conservation**. We just can't produce and distribute it properly! The elimination of scarcity is fully proven in Peter Diamadis's and Steven Kolter's *Abundance*. However, we need to understand the ingredients that allow the pie to exist and how those ingredients make the current conflicts important to the global picture. I will describe the solutions in U.S. terms, but they apply to the global economy.

Let me state this loud and clear: *the macroeconomic systems of the world are in need of change!* The proper macroeconomic philosophy will free the politicians from fighting about philosophy, and it will allow them to argue and compromise over the specifics of implementation. **The debate between the 19ᵗʰ Century Laissez-faire Libertarian economics and the 20ᵗʰ Century Keynesian Economics has gone on long enough! Both are not complete enough to create a 21ˢᵗ Century Win-Win Economy.** I will take the most successful parts from each philosophy and add to them the proper money creation and distribution systems.

The political economic debate that continually splits our country and our leaders is a vicious cycle that can be stopped. Arguments over tax and spend (fiscal policy), and the so-called national debt are not the answer to our economic problems. Fiscal policy was not the cause of the "Great

Recession," "Great Depression," or any other economic downturn; therefore, it *cannot be the solution!* What is the solution? I have one.

This book is not an exhaustive description and defense of capitalism. There are plenty of economists who have expounded on this subject. Instead, I will define Capitalism and provide the structures to reduce its major flaws. The solutions will not be about zero or limited government, but the *"right"* government. One of my goals is to educate our leaders and to empower the government to be a more efficient partner so we can accomplish the necessary programs to insure our future. My answers will be based on imperfect human operations, not on nonexistent human perfections.

This is not a proposal to solve all the problems of mankind, just the economic ones. The book is not a proposal for some creation of Utopia or what I call "La-La Land". These are solutions that I believe we should and can do *now*, not in the next century. **This book only covers and defends with economic reasoning and history—not on moral, fairness, political, community or social justice. These are valid points, but should not be used until an economic defense is presented.**

In my many talks and articles over the decades, I am either labeled a "righty" by the left or a "lefty" by the right. This means that I probably have it just right. This is why I have two separate titles for my same speech. For the right, it is labeled **"Saving Capitalism"** and for the left it is called **"Progressive Economics".** The solutions that I propose are nonpartisan; they are purely based on economic logic and reasoning. So keep an open mind!

This is a **solutions book** written for the average citizen, but should be read by academics. In order for the book to be of reasonable length, it is not a typical academic book. It is not written in what I call "Econo-speak". I will try to keep the language easy to understand, and I will also provide a glossary. There will be mainly answers provided, with a limited amount of descriptive history, examples, footnotes, and statistics.

I will refer to books and websites for you to read as a way of providing additional evidence, validation, economic reasoning and examples. Unfortunately, we cannot discuss every economic problem in detail; however, a general macroeconomic roadmap for decision making and basic solutions are provided within.

There are six sections in this book; the first four sections are based on the *four major flaws* of capitalism. I will provide specific solutions to overcome the negative effects of each flaw. The most important of all the flaws is the fallacy that money is scarce, which we will discuss in the first section. In the second section, we will discuss the conflict between microeconomics and macroeconomics, which results in not creating enough customers. In the third section, we will cover insufficient competition. The fourth section will cover long-range profits versus short-term profits. These four major flaws are all interconnected; they are organized in order of importance. The fifth section covers short messages on an array of macroeconomic topics including trade, taxes, environment, healthcare, education, usury, and regulations. In the last section you will find a summary of recommendations that has to be debated and implemented.

In the **gradual** implementation of these recommendations to reduce the major flaws of capitalism, we will create winners in our country and around the globe. There are answers to solve our problems, but we have difficulty implementing them, mainly because we lack the proper macroeconomic philosophy. The following paragraphs are a description of the results of implementing the win-win recommendations.

The populace will have their basic living requirements and education met with reasonable work and opportunities to advance and to grow as individuals. Just think of the morality of it! This will prepare them for the evolutionary **"Robotic Age". With more money and personal time, it will unlock the human potential of a great number of our very talented people to solve our problems.** The global stability this brings will reduce the many conflicts we have around the world.

Large and small businesses will have substantially more sales from the increase in the number of affluent customers, clients, consumers and citizens. Businesses will have more profits as a result of the lower cost of labor, and a lack of pressure to raise wages. Businesses will provide more innovation with less regulation. The substantial increase in personal time will rapidly expand industries such as entertainment, education, travel, sports, charity, arts, and wellness. These industries will usher in the **"Personal Growth Age"**.

Commercial banks will be winners by not having an unsustainable system that periodically collapses or has severe write-downs. They will have substantial profits from their continued banking business as well as the operations of the many new distribution systems of new money. They will have an abundance of deposits as they replace treasuries because these are federally insured deposits. The private investment banks and financial advisors will have more money to manage and the financial service industry will boom.

Our environment will start to improve as the elimination of scarce money is used to convert the source of energy from fossil fuels to alternatives and provide funds for prevention and clean up, especially in our rivers and oceans. Infrastructure repair will accelerate. It will allow the implementation of the five Rs: Reuse, Repair, Renewables, Regeneration and Recycling. Other funds will be used to provide research and development to cure cancer, malaria and other diseases. New exploration will then proceed in our oceans and space.

These solutions are neither socialistic nor utopian. There will always be human disparity, differences and conflicts. We will still fight over operational decisions but the basic macroeconomic philosophy will be established!

Chapter 2

CAPITALISM

Let's start by describing some benefits of capitalism, because most of this book is about improving it and taking it to the next level—to a *Win-Win 21st Century Economy*. My definition of capitalism: the first choice for the delivery of goods and services to the people is through a *private ownership operation in a competitive marketplace*. We need to increase competition to increase quality of goods and services, employment, stimulate innovation, and increase research and development, while reducing regulations and inflation. If business operations cannot be subject to a competitive marketplace, we have to consider other alternatives for delivery. Nonprofits, government owned firms, and substantially increasing regulations, including price controls, could be alternatives to business monopolies.

In the history of humankind, there has never been a period where vast majorities of the people have lived a superior quality of life as in the last 70 years in Europe, the USA, and Japan; we can also see increases in developing nations. The lower middle class has a quality of life that in many ways is better than the elite had 150 years ago. My definition of equality is having adequate healthcare, nutrition, education and shelter, along with the opportunity for advancement. It is not the standard definition which would describe the gap in income or net worth between the rich and the poor. **The current system has delivered basic living benefits and opportunities to advance to many. Now it is time to deliver them to everyone on this globe.** This is accomplished by reducing the effects of the four major flaws of capitalism. The U.S. economy was well under way to solving these flaws when we started a reactionary course, in the 1980's, back to some concept of the "free market place solves all" (libertarian, laissez-faire philosophies).

There is no such thing as a free market place; there is always some undue influence somewhere. The free market ideology *assumes human perfection*, which by nature cannot exist. All markets are subject to distortions of non-market variables, such as religious practices, local customs, and traditional laws, oligarchic, ethnic, or national factors including government regulations. In practice, every market is planned and organized by some party; this has been so ever since the Neolithic rhythms of agriculture planting and harvesting. In today's world, governments design, organize, enforce, and help fund the ever-changing market place! In fact, there can be no fair and competitive marketplace without governments. A marketplace today may be an abstract location like a fleeting digital connection. The marketplace can have deeper processes than a mere exchange of goods and services. Any totally unregulated marketplace will eventually cease to exist, as it becomes a monopoly or at best an oligopoly. Civilization is defined by rules; rules create markets, and governments generate rules. See Robert Reich's recent book *Saving Capitalism,* for its discussion on markets and the powers to influence them.

Human imperfections exist in all operations, both government and nongovernment. Since government inefficiencies are exposed by the press, one has to review the errors of the private sector. Professor Ha-Joon Chang's book, *Things They Don't Tell You About Capitalism*, is a *must read* depicting the many failures in the private sector.

Chapter 3

POLITICS

This book is not about the money power in politics and how it influences governments. The wealthy individuals and businesses involved in politics through lobbying and political donations set and skew the rules to their perceived self-interests. **My concern is that their macroeconomic influence is at best misguided but mostly wrong, especially in the long run. This book is about correcting the macroeconomic philosophy of the 1%, so that they will use their influence correctly to create a win-win economy.** In our society, "money talks", so they are the stewards of protecting our smaller businesses, customers and clients. It is in their best interests!

The extensive power of wealth gained by lobbying, campaign contributions, and jurisdictional girth will probably not be countered until some form of public financing of elections can be implemented. The "Clean Money" movement has created the appropriate structures for having both transparency of private and public financing of elections.

Have you ever wondered why you continually see changes in democratically elected governments from right to left and from left to right, and then switching back again? You see this on a global scope, not just in the USA. Were those leaders so incompetent that the electorate had to change back and forth? In the UK, they elected a conservative party and then skipped over the liberal party to another liberal party to form a government. In Egypt, they kicked out a right leaning dictator, voted in a left leaning Muslim and were so unhappy with the economy and his governance they forced him out, too. We also see the switches from right to left continually throughout South America. What is going on here?

The general population always wants to see a thriving economy and a quality standard of living, or at least an improving one with opportunities for advancement. Why are those leaders not delivering? Why can't they govern? The reason is, the leaders are not in control of the major influence on the economy regarding the amount of money in circulation or the money supply. *Money in circulation is the life-blood of any economy.* If money in circulation is reduced too much and/or overly concentrated in the hands of a few, there will be a recession/depression. A quality economy needs to have money flowing and diversified in many different hands.

Therefore, monetary reform should be on top of the agenda for debate. However, it is not even on the agenda or even discussed in the campaigns. Why isn't monetary reform the major economic issue? The first reason is the hidden nature of *what money is* and *how it is created.* The second reason is the *ignorance* and failure of our leaders to read and become educated about the origins of money. The third reason is the amount of money the banking sector contributes to campaigns and to lobbying. The fourth reason is the major influence in the macroeconomic academia of *neoclassical philosophy.* A majority of economic professor's formulas and models have money as a minor or neutral factor, but in reality, it is the *major factor!* The fifth reason is the *fear of change,* any change, always hinders any debate and implementation. Therefore, any reform proposals have to have a win-win scenario or the powerful banking industry will stop it in its tracks. Most of the current proposals are too far left to get the time of day by the right. We start with this topic in Section I.

I label businessmen—whose mindset is on microeconomics not macroeconomics—as the "business right". They call themselves fiscal conservatives, which is a micro term not a macro term. The "business right" still evaluates the entire economy the same way they consider an individual business or industry. It is almost the complete opposite. The goal of an individual business or industry is to maximize profits either over the short run or the long run. Therefore, one of business management's major objectives is to reduce cost, of which labor is one of them. These managers consider the vast global labor pool as another market or commodity. The labor pool cannot be completely subject to supply and demand, because a quality economy (macroeconomics) needs to have a substantial amount of well-paid customers and clients. An example of this implementation will be explained in Section II with Henry Ford's pioneer solution.

Chapter 4

INEQUALITY

The new hot topic is *inequality* and how it is increasing. This is a very vague term. We are human beings with substantial differences; we cannot all be Donald Trump, Bill Gates, or Warren Buffet. We are too imperfect to create a utopia or all to have the same standard of living. It is just not possible at this time in human evolution.

There are many reasons why inequality exists in the economy. Before I give my specific list, I will review the general macroeconomic reasons. One, we are NOT created equal! We have many different talents, abilities, and appearances along with unique emotional and physical make-ups. Second, the institution of capitalism—competitive markets by their very nature, naturally flow money to the wealthy. The main reason for this flow is that *it is easier to make more money if you already have money*. This goes for businesses as well as individuals. This naturally causes a shift towards business consolidation creating monopolies and oligopolies.

For those doubters, I have never seen a statistical, economic study proving otherwise. If you do a little macroeconomic historical reading covering the last 175 years, you can see this yourself. Inequality was proved again by the recent bestsellers by Thomas Picketty, *Capitalism in the Twenty-First Century* and *Inequality* by Anthony Atkinson.

The nature of capitalism eventually causes so much consolidation of wealth that the entire economy or country becomes unstable. This instability could cause a complete breakdown in society because of a lack of basic survival goods for the general population. This failure can even result in severe violence and/or revolution. This growing income disparity is not only a disaster for the poor, but also a threat to the rich. Poverty breeds broken families, crime and criminal organizations, beggars, prostitution, mass immigration, social protest movements, and failed states. The most recent examples are Egypt and the Arab Spring. These societal upheavals would probably not have occurred so swiftly if they had a reasonable standard of living and opportunities for advancement. You can also see the failures in our own economy in 1907, 1929, and 2008.

The following is my list of additional reasons for inequality:

1. Birth – 41% of individuals in the USA remain in the same income level they were born in.
2. Lack of Education
3. Lack of access to capital for investing and savings
4. Lack of luck – This one is more important than you think
5. Overreliance on debt
6. Lack of adequate wages
7. Employment in the wrong industry or profession
8. Competition against extremely low cost or slave labor
9. Productivity – replaced by machines
10. Caught in the boom/bust economy which hurts the middle and lower income class
11. Lack of competition because of monopolies and oligopolies— less jobs
12. Illegalities and discrimination

Therefore, my definition of equality is: all having an opportunity to advance with adequate health care, education, shelter, and nutrition. The definition also includes the right to live in a sustainable environment with drinkable water and breathable air. There are currently billions of people on this globe that do not meet my definition. This book will illustrate the specific solutions to solve this global inequality both on a private and governmental level. We can create a whole new populace of quality customers, clients, consumers, and citizens resulting in a permanent boom and quality of life for all.

Our concern should be how well the populace is living, not how much the top is making. The exception being the extreme consolidation of inherited wealth that is among several thousand families worldwide. This is not about a safety net for the unemployed or those who need welfare. This is about providing the basic necessities of life for all! It is not measured by GDP-growth! (See Section V – Statistics) **We do not want to eliminate competitive markets.** Instead, these markets provide for more freedom, diversity of investments, and checks and balances over government. **Governments cannot do it all.**

We are all in this economy together; what happens to one group economically effects all. We are now in a globalized economy—good, bad, or indifferent. Therefore, our solutions are for the globe at large and each country individually. There are substantial numbers of projects that need to be accomplished to advance humankind, such as space exploration, medical advances, and environmental issues. **Reducing the flaws of capitalism will allow us to move forward in solving our problems and enhancing mankind by creating the correct win-win political macroeconomic philosophy.**

Chapter 5

LIBERTARIANISM

Since the current Republican debates discuss "limited or no government," I thought I would discuss the macroeconomic history of laissez faire – libertarianism of the last 150 years. This philosophy has many followers because it sounds simple and accurate. Unfortunately, this is far from the truth and it actually fails in practice. These long-term failures can only be observed over a period of decades, not years. Libertarians fail to understand the proper definition of money, its unlimited demand, how money is created, and its infusion into the economy. The problem with laissez-faire economics is that the wealth generated at the top does not trickle down to the rest of society to a sufficient extent. It does not employ enough people nor pay them adequately to keep the system going.

In the latter half of the 19th Century, the U.S. had no income taxes, anti-trust laws, effective unions, minimum wages, Federal Reserve, nor any fiscal spending programs such as Welfare, Medicare and Social Security. The U.S. had the most economically non-involved Federal government that was physically possible. This lack of economic government involvement resulted in an extreme concentration of individual wealth and large business monopolies. Approximately 4,500 families owned most of the wealth in the country. Yes, it was still better than most other countries at the time. Because of this concentration and lack of money, there were severe recessions-panics in 1837, 1857, 1873, 1873-79, 1892-6, 1904 and 1907, culminating in the Great Depression of the 1930's.

In 1933, President Franklin Roosevelt implemented a Keynesian macroeconomic philosophy, which promoted government spending to stimulate demand. The U.S. then began getting the government involved in the economy with domestic spending programs. These policies still did not get us into a healthy economy until the largest government spending programs of World War II, followed by the Federal Highway System and the GI Bill which gave free education and reasonable home loans to veterans. This spending created the best economy in the history of the world.

Even now, governments, especially the U.S., invest in basic research, commercialization and early stage financing of companies to create entirely new markets and sectors. These markets include the Internet, nanotechnology, biotechnology, pharmaceuticals, and clean energy. The government has also invested in companies like Apple, Google, Intel, Compaq, and Tesla, just to name a few. The investments in basic research are where private companies do not want to take the risk, but, instead, piggyback off the government's efforts. Many private companies then utilize the government's direct financing of their firms through loans and grants. A complete discussion of government investments with examples can be found in Mariana Mazzucato's new book, *The Entrepreneurial State*, where she also proves that the government does not get enough return on their investment from just taxing these companies.

Government programs were surely not perfect, but were always trying to improve. The government really had only one major flaw to correct; that of a very under diversified, unfair monetary system, which will be discussed in Section I. In the 1980's the Reagan Administration reintroduced the 19th Century failed Laissez-faire macroeconomic philosophy instead of improving on the policies of the previous 50 years. This gradual shift backward away from Keynesian's philosophy eventually culminated in the "Great Recession of 2008". Instead of giving billions to the U.S. headquartered auto manufactures, we could have given longer term and lower cost loans to consumers to stimulate the purchase of hundreds of thousands of unsold new cars. This is "trickle up" economics. The gross profits and cash flow would have ended up back in the auto companies with consumers ending up with newer, more fuel efficient cars. A win-win scenario. This also holds true for the trillions of dollars in mortgages.

The Libertarians argue that there was still too much government involved in the 19th Century economy and that the free market place is self-correcting. This argument has two major flaws. One, there is no clear definition of a "free" market nor do the same standard rules exist for a marketplace. There are many types of markets with differing human influences and operations. The second flaw, the major one, is that a "free" market concept assumes that humans and their commercial interactions are perfect. There is no such thing as human perfection either individually or in our institutions.

Therefore, this libertarian philosophy does us an extreme disservice by always saying "no government" instead of "the right government"!

The following is a list of some of the reactionary policies, implemented in the last 30 years that have hurt the economy:

1. Reducing anti-trust enforcement creating many new monopolies and oligopolies which reduce competition in the market place.
2. Eliminating the Glass-Steagall Act of 1933 separating the money creators (commercial banks) from the money managers (investment banks), which was one of the causes of the worst financial crisis in modern history.
3. Reducing the enforcement of financial regulations that made the financial crisis even worse.
4. Hindering raises of the minimum wage, reducing Union participation, and sending jobs to Asia. This outsourcing of jobs reduced the quantity and quality of customers, clients and consumers. This created excessive borrowing just to keep up a normal standard of living.

So here we are! What do we do? I do **not** recommend going to a more socialistic state. Socialism is a political economic doctrine that unlike capitalism is based on government ownership of production and distribution or collective ownership by all the people in that country. We have seen the failures of socialism in the totalitarian governments like the Soviet Union, China, Cuba, and democracies like Venezuela, India and Israel. Socialism, the opposite of libertarianism, also assumes that humans operate perfectly. I propose the improvement of the capitalistic system by reducing the effects of its major flaws. Government spending on welfare, social security, research and development is **not** socialism because they do not own the means of production or distribution. **This means that government spending is "consumerism" not socialism.** This spending makes for a superior economy by having better customers and clients.

SECTION I

Not Enough Money—The Big One!

"When money flows, we grow, and when it stops, we flop."

Chapter 6

WHAT IS MONEY & WHAT IS NOT MONEY?

In my discussions and presentations over the decades, I have discovered that the concept of money is very mysterious to most people. The current system is too confusing, nontransparent, and unsustainable to provide an understanding of what money is and how it comes about; it has been the most difficult challenge in the monetary reform movement.

The correct definition of money goes back to Aristotle believe it or not! He wrote: "Money exists not by nature but by law". All of today's money is fiat money, meaning there is no asset backing its value. It is created out of thin air and is mostly a digital entry; not printed currency. It costs zero to create—just a simple push of a computer key! The current money supply is made up of 97% digital entries, only 3% is actual cash currency. Money has value because people work together in an economy under a legal framework. Paying one's taxes helps legitimize a fiat currency, which is issued by a government, and has no actual asset backing it. There is no longer any country that has a gold reserve backing its currency.

Money is not a commodity like gold. It is also not credit or debt—even though that is how it is created and distributed in today's world! It is the lifeblood of an economy. It is needed for purchases and investments instead of barter. It is a medium of exchange. If money is scarce, you can count on a recession or depression. When money substantially flows, circulates and is dispersed, you will see a very healthy economy—even if there is some excess inflation. Just look at the most recent experience of India. After removing only two currency notes from circulation, India experienced extreme economic havoc.

Individuals use money for spending and savings, as well as for investing for future spending (retirement). It is a record of their productive work. Businesses use it for current operations and capital expenditures to advance their business. It is part of wealth and a storehouse of value.

Governments use it for current spending for their various programs. They all have faith in their money that it will not inflate away. Money needs to be the *servant* of commerce, *not* the *master*, as it basically is now.

Money is currently generated and distributed into the economy through the monetary system. **This system is made up of commercial and central banks that create the new money by making loans.** The first usage of newly created money in the economy is called "new money". After the first use, the money becomes "old money", which *continues to circulate* in the economy. The term "old money" does not refer to the term that describes traditionally wealthy families. This section has nothing to do with old money! This also means that it has little to do with the private financial services sector, where I built my practice as a Certified Financial Planner, only the commercial banking system. **The cost of creating money is ZERO! The cost of distribution is small. Money does not have to be scarce!**

Chapter 7

HISTORY OF MONETARY SYSTEMS AROUND THE WORLD

Most countries, big and small, A to Z, Argentina to Zimbabwe, have had significant monetary-banking crises in the last half-century. I am not going into their history, but the following is a short list: Germany, Hungary, Czech Republic, Bulgaria, Estonia, Poland, Russia, Sweden, Chile, Mexico, Venezuela, Indonesia, Korea, India, Turkey, Thailand, and Bolivia, just to name a few.

In the last 30 years, the world has suffered six globally significant financial crises:

- Latin America debt crisis of the early 1980s
- Japanese crisis of the 1990s
- The Tequila crisis of 1994, whose epicenter was Mexico, but also affected many parts of Latin America
- East Asian crisis of 1997-1999
- Global financial crisis of 2007-2009; started by the U.S.
- Eurozone financial crisis 0f 2010-2013; and the ongoing Greek tragedy

According to Martin Wolf in his book, *The Shifts and Shocks*, "the Euro has been a disaster! A project intended to strengthen solidarity, bring prosperity, and weaken the German economic domination of Europe has achieved precisely the opposite. It has undermined solidarity, destroyed prosperity, and reinforced German domination, at least for a while."

The following is a review of U.S. monetary history up to the enactment of the Federal Reserve in 1913. The English Crown took away the Colonial States' right to create and spend their colonial currency. This caused a severe depression in the colonies and was the major cause of the Revolutionary War, according to Ben Franklin in his autobiography. Then the Continental Congress, to fund the Revolutionary War, issued their currency. Soon after, British warships in the New York harbor were

20

found printing massive amounts of counterfeits in an effort to destroy the new currency. This was s tactic of the British at that time.

After the establishment of our nation, there was significant political conflict to establish a National Bank. Two acts were passed, creating the first and second National Banks. President Andrew Jackson eliminated the bank and was right to do so. However, he did not replace it with any money creating system, causing the severe depression of 1837. (Note – this was the last time the national debt was paid off.)

Abraham Lincoln had to finance the Civil War, and the U.S. private bankers wanted to loan the money to the government at a significant interest rate. Lincoln then established the very successful "greenbacks" where the government just printed up the money and paid for the war. **(This gives us the best example that money does not have to be created by a loan/debt.)** After the Civil War, the bankers wanted to take the greenbacks out of circulation to reduce the competition from government created currency. Every time the government takes money out of circulation, a recession is created. They were called "panics" in those days.

In summary of our nation's first 150 years, the immature monetary system and consequent lack of a fiscal system (tax & spend) created the panics of 1837, 1857, 1873, 1893, 1907; the Banking Crisis of 1884; the recessions of 1892-1896, 1904, and 1921 and the severe depression from 1873 to 1879.

When you review monetary history, every country, and I mean *every* country, has gone through these significant crises. In our nation's last 100 years, the under diversified monetary system and lack of fiscal spending (recirculation) in the U.S. created the severe Great Depression of the 1930's; post World War II recessions in the 50's, 80's and 90's; culminating in the current Great Recession, which began in 2007. This was caused by the monetary subprime collapse, which we spread to other parts of the world. Why was this necessary? This Great Recession was caused solely by the private commercial banking system's mortgage departments. These banks also loaned funds to the private mortgage companies. The crash was made more severe by the investment banks, and lack of financial regulation enforcement and improper incentives. **The 2008 Great Recession had nothing to do with the fiscal policy (tax & spend) of government!**

Some of the other governments involved in the subprime crisis were in surplus not deficit. Then the crash hit, causing tax revenues to decrease and safety net expenses (unemployment insurance) to increase. On top of that, most European governments had to bail out their commercial banks. Their central bank did not bail them out as was done by the U.S. Federal Reserve. Now the European Central Bank is getting around to supporting the European commercial banks with their quantitative easing.

Chapter 8

THE CURRENT MONETARY SYSTEM

December 23, 2013 marked the 100th Anniversary of the Federal Reserve Act, which created the Central Bank for the United States. The Federal Reserve is called a central bank. Other important central banks are: The Bank of Japan, The Bank of England, and the European Union's Central Bank. These central banks are basically the fourth branch of government, *which has more influence on the economy than tax and spend (fiscal policy).*

The Federal Reserve is **NOT** a federal agency. It is primarily a private agency that regulates commercial banks. These commercial banks generate the majority of our money in circulation. The Federal Reserve is **NOT** a reserve; it directly creates the rest of our money supply by a stroke of a computer key. In its 100 years of existence, we have had 16 recessions, the Great Depression, the Great Recession, and excess inflationary periods creating extensive human hardships. *It is time to end these extreme downturns or at least make them less severe.* Increasing and/or changing banking regulations and breaking up or **nationalizing** the banks is **not** a substitution for reform, as it does not alter the unsustainable system by leaving monetary creation with the banks. In fact, there have been many government owned banks that experience the same failures as privately owned banks. Many central banks are actually owned by the government such as the Bank of Japan and the Bank of England. **We need a 21st Century, modern monetary system to create a quality Win-Win economy!**

The major source of new money in an economy is generated by the commercial banking system, i.e. Wells Fargo, Citibank, Bank of America, Chase, and the smaller local banks. They don't loan out your deposits. They loan out far more. This excess is new money created out of thin air! This is a very important concept to understand. This is called "debt" money—where new money is created and distributed by only a loan.

Congress gave the power to the Federal Reserve in 1913, to operate the monetary system. This system creates new money *only by issuing debt –* private and government. **Private debt-money is only created by the commercial bank loans** under the regulation of the Federal Reserve. Government debt money is only created directly by the Federal Reserve's open market operations, at the Fed's bank in New York. The Fed gradually buys U.S Treasuries from the banks with newly created money. **This is forced money creation by issuing Treasuries to fund deficit spending. This is called, "Monetization of the Debt."**

Basically, someone—or government—has to go into debt to release new money into the economy. This is the main reason you see a very slow recovery and growth when we have a financial collapse like 2008. In reality, there is no cost of creating new money except for creating too much in circulation, thus creating excess or hyperinflation. Creating too little with narrow circulation severely costs the economy in recessions, depressions, and extreme human hardships. In reality, there should be no cost for creating new money; there should only be the nominal cost for distribution.

When commercial banking lending slows down or freezes up, as in 2008, new money ceases to be issued and is reduced at the same time, whereby the lesser system of money creation takes over. This lesser system is deficit spending by the Federal government. **Yes, deficit spending forces the Federal Reserve to create money by monetizing the debt. They digitally create money (a touch of the computer keys) and buy Treasuries and other assets from commercial banks. No, it is not all borrowed from China.** The newer policy of buying other assets from commercial banks started as a result of the 2008 crash. This is called **quantitative easing**, which basically creates new money by buying the suspect mortgages that the banks still hold. This process of monetizing the debt is a substitute or an addition for the lack of money in circulation from the banking system. Federal spending is also more diversified in its distribution. Deficit spending has kept us out of severe depression! There was no fiscal spending in 1929 and the Federal Reserve tightened money, which caused the Great Depression.

The next question is: When do you reduce this substantial deficit spending? If reduced too early, as Japan did in 1997 and the U.S. did in 1937, the country goes back into recession. This reduction of deficit spending is labeled "austerity".

The following example gives you a brief overview of the steps involved in creating money under our current system of government debt. The U.S. Government needs $1,000 to pay the salary of a federal employee. The U.S. Treasury issues a $1,000 Treasury Note, Bill, or Bond to the private government bond brokers for sale. This note is then purchased by commercial banks. The check is recorded by the Fed as a liability against the government, and the Note becomes an asset of the Fed.

The Fed has created the $1000 check with simple keystrokes on their computer without actually getting the money from any specific place. In other words, the Fed issued this money against no funds of its own. Thus we see why many call this money creation process "money created out of nothing or thin air". This is also called "**fiat money**", which all countries use. It is in reality, **debt money, debt backed money or bank money.**

The process for making a loan by commercial banks, which is the largest source of new money, is called a *fractional reserve system.* This system allows a bank to create new money on a fraction of deposits made with that bank. This fraction is determined by the Federal Reserve Board, as part of its monetary policy, and is called the *reserve requirement.* If the reserve requirement is 10%, then the banking system can loan $900 from the deposit of the $1000 salary check or 90% of the value of the $1000. This new $900 loan is then deposited in another bank, which can make another $810 loan. This process repeats itself until a maximum of $9000 is loaned out by the commercial banks from the initial deposit of $1000.

25

All the new money created was created out of nothing; or to describe the process more correctly, it was created using debt. Therefore, it can be labeled debt backed money. (With the merger of commercial and investment banks and loans driving the creation process, the supposed restrictions provided by the reserve requirement are very limited.) In other words, every loan or overdraft creates money and every repayment of these financial instruments destroys money.

In reality, banks issue the loans first, creating deposits in the process, and then they look for reserves by raising capital, deposits, or borrowing from the Federal Reserve. Therefore, it is almost pure credit money, not fractional reserve creation, much of which was created for themselves for their trading departments—investment banks attached to their commercial banks—because of the cancellation of the Glass-Steagall Act, which separated the commercial banks from the investment banks. In other words, they violate their own rules. This process is intentionally kept invisible!

There is no reason for you to comprehend all the lingo and complicated operations of the Federal Reserve System. It is just the gyrations of a faulty, incomplete and monopolistic system to issue and control the supply of money in circulation. The point is that you know about its basic function of "new" money creation and distribution.

The big questions are: If all money is created through debt principle, where does the money come from to pay the **compound** interest charges by these banks? Where is it written that we have to create and distribute money only through debt? **Nowhere!** This debt system of money creation and distribution has been going on since about the 12th Century. My audiences have always asked me, "Why have they not changed this unsustainable system by now?" There are many reasons:

- People are reluctant to change
- The banking system is very opaque and politically powerful

- The academic world is dominated by the neoclassical philosophy, which has money as a *minor* or neutral factor in their theories and formulas; but in reality, it is the *major* factor
- "Illusion of reality", coined by Daniel Kahneman, is the irrational behavior of doing the same thing over and over and expecting different results
- Because the debt money system has been around since the 12th century, it has become a religious belief

Truths about Money

1. Debt (loans) is the only way we currently get new money into circulation
2. **Money is not scarce!** It takes a simple push of a computer keyboard to create
3. The **cost of this creation is ZERO ($0)** except for excess inflation. There is a small cost for distribution
4. **There is no such thing as the "National Debt".** A debt is something that has to be paid back. The U.S. has not paid its national debt off since 1835. **The debt should be labeled as the: National Monetization account or the National Monetization debt account. This type of debt is not the same as you and I owing money!** The only way the debt is really retired is by the Federal Reserve Bank of New York creating new money and buying Treasuries. People think that it is still an obligation of the U.S. government, but it is too large to be paid back by increasing taxes and cutting expenses. The Treasuries are also automatically rolled over to new treasuries on maturity. The National Debt is not going to be paid back by taxes! Over half of the debt is sitting as reserves and investments in commercial and central banks, the Social Security trust fund, insurance companies, and sovereign and pension funds. Also, money is over concentrated in the 1%. This over concentration is one reason for the current low inflation

5. **The current Great Recession was 100% caused by the private money system,** *not the tax and spend fiscal system*!

6. There is no historical evidence of excess inflation caused by direct government currency issue occurring in the U.S. (18th & 19th century.) Remember, the global excess or hyperinflationary incidences in the last 100 years have occurred with the current debt money system in place, including asset bubbles. According to research by Rogoff and Reinhart in their book: *This Time Is Different,* the inflationary rate was higher in the 20th century than the 19th century

7. There is no such thing as a "business cycle for an entire economy". It is a monetary cycle

8. The economy cannot grow enough to pay off the enormous compounding debt. No increase in taxes or decrease in spending can pay off this enormous amount of compounding. The global private and public debt is three times larger than the entire world economy.

9. Taxes do **not** compete with the private sector because the government spends it right back into the economy. **What competes with the private sector is the sucking sound that is made when the excessive compounding interest charge of money creation moves out of private sector (Main Street) into the financial banking sector (Wall Street)!**

Chapter 9

REASONS FOR REFORM

The following reasons, not in order of importance, will hopefully convince you that we need evolutionary monetary reform by eliminating private debt creation of money, with a substantial increase in the number of distribution systems. This is, by far, the major economic issue that needs to be resolved in order to create a 21st Century Win-Win Economy:

1. Diversification dilutes the power that any one system brings to monetary creation. It eliminates the benefits of monetary creation only going to a few private citizens and one sector of the economy. Why should only one financial industry system of commercial banking have the *monopolistic* power of money creation and infusion when there is an unlimited demand? **Wouldn't you like to have your own printing press in your basement?**

2. In reality, the current system of higher interest rates to control the money supply punishes the weakest, smallest players first and most severely, while the largest and more powerful enterprises are able to withstand the increased cost. The major reasons for business failures are: too much competition, mismanagement, and a lack of capital. The latter being the most common

3. **Controlling the monetary supply based on interest punishes the entire economy. It should be controlled by volume, geography and industry, guided by inflationary statistics. These decisions can now be made easier with our current computer power**

4. Diversification reduces banking favoritism, nepotism, bribes, political cronyism, shoddy management, criminal activity, and increases transparency.

5. The boom/bust scenario we see in various assets, industries, and regions will be greatly reduced by not over lending in successful industries, companies, and individuals. It makes managing risks less difficult. The current dilemma of regulation is that it is difficult to deal with borrowers when life is good. Who tells the banks not to lend to real estate when real estate is the hottest part of the economy and running up great profits? Or shipping? Or oil and gas? Or high tech? Having other systems with different objectives will more effectively control over lending, thereby reducing boom/bust scenarios within an industry or an entire economy

6. Diversification gives more capitalistic opportunities to others, creating more owners and increasing competition, while at the same time reducing human hardship and **inequality.** This means growth! Offsetting one of the other major flaws of capitalism that is, "not enough competition" Section III. The current system of bank creation of new money goes 70%+ to real estate mortgages both residential and nonresidential

7. Diversification expands investment of new money, based on the *ability to succeed* and not solely on the *ability to repay.* It is also based on the quality of your talent and the need for your enterprise, rather than focusing only on the quantity of your collateral

8. Diversification reduces the effects of any over lending during economic expansion. This means that the new distribution systems can divert new money from industries that do not need it, to those who do. This allows for more lending and investing on the monetary expansion/inflation side of the equation rather than implementing a contraction. The end result is a lesser chance of recession/depression

9. Excessive wide range defaults and bankruptcies (domestic or foreign) will not hurt the entire monetary system as much, because the monetary system is spread among many distribution systems with lesser amounts of money in each rather than a

single banking system. Therefore, the monetary system will have less stress due to economic volatility. In fact, bankruptcies, defaults, and write-downs are the only ways money remains in the economy *permanently*, because when **a bank loan is repaid, it reduces the money in circulation**

10. Diversity and transparency help control the amounts of new money issued for aggregate consumer demand (credit card, auto loans and mortgages) versus loans to businesses increasing the supply of goods and services. Having more control of the quality and quantity of new money being issued results in less chance of an over expansive money supply that creates an asset or consumer bubble economy.

11. Diversity can provide more capital to areas with high need, such as low-tech industries, environmental businesses, and lower income areas. Diversification provides more funds for investment

12. Monetary policy is an art not a science! Monetary policy requires judgment at every stage of the process, from the initial formulation to the final implementation. Judgment is susceptible to human error. If there is an error in the one major system, like the 2008 mortgage crash, it can lead to tragic consequences. With more diversified delivery systems, there is less of a chance any single judgment error will cause a substantial financial collapse

13. The fiscal systems operate on a much more diversified basis. There are many governments—federal, county, and city. In those governments, there are many delivery systems—military, police, fire, Medicare, Social Security, education, and welfare, both social and corporate. Why shouldn't new money be more diversified?

14. Credit risk formulas and models currently used by the private commercial banks, which are inherently flawed, will be reduced because some of new money distribution is moved to other private distribution systems and the government. Continuing to

improve and increase regulation and risk models helps, but it is not the answer! Reckless lending will be scattered and there will be fewer defaults, especially with the use of an equity component rather than all debt

15. A key element in the art of monetary policy is *coping with change*. The current most important change is *accelerating globalization*. Again, with more transparency and decision-making based on the volume of money created using diversified distribution systems, it will be easier and safer to cope with change

16. We need transparency and diversity to reduce the negative effects of excessive greed

17. The central banks attempt to have many regulations and capital requirements in order to offset factors of self-interest and other human frailties. But with the delivery basically in one system with reduced transparency, any errors that do get through are certainly overly accentuating the negatives, i.e., sub-prime mortgages

18. Our single, private, commercial banking system is less and less willing to share risk. It has lost the ability to foster the development of novel or non-standardized risky, private enterprise. This means that economic development slows and future generations are disadvantaged

19. Banking crises will not be as detrimental to the overall economy and other financial systems because these crises will not be as severe or as influential in the monetary-financial sector. Consequently, human hardships will be greatly reduced

20. Diversification reduces the "herd behavior" of financial institutions and investors in whatever country or market is fashionable at the moment. Herd behavior can lead into excessive bank lending and over borrowing within a particular industry, country, or group of countries

21. Diversification will make the repeal of the Glass-Steagall Act less important as the power to control large quantities of new

money will be lessened, reducing the ability of the commercial banks to lend to their investment banks (trading departments) which control and manipulate markets. It will also reduce the amounts that can be invested in risky options and derivatives substantially reducing risk to the entire banking system

22. The current system charges excessive interest (usury) and unfairly transfers income from investors, workers, and owners to the banking sector, resulting in a lower level of production and investment to the detriment of the economy. **Removing the monetary creation process from the banks and increasing the diversity of distribution provides more support for the real economy (Main Street) rather than the financial sector (Wall Street). It also increases competition and reduces inequality.** This means that the monetary system funds new means of production, not just collateral-based lending

23. **Reduction of the tax burden** on a vast majority of the population. This is a direct result of paying for some federal government programs with newly created dollars. A diversification of systems will infuse more money into the economy, resulting in an expansive economy, causing greater total tax revenues with lower tax rates except for the top 1%

24. Having the monetary system providing for some spending programs substantially reduces the political fiscal pressures of balancing budgets

25. **If all the debt and interest had to be paid off at once,** there would not be enough money in circulation because the current money-debt system does not create the compounding interest charges, but only the principle. Since it does not have to be paid off at once, there is enough money in circulation to pay interest, but it does create unnecessary scarcity that causes hardships, conflicts, and additional borrowings to pay the debt service. This limits growth by forcing the economy to keep borrowing in order to pay the interest charges. This is the main reason that the banking system is unsustainable. It is impossible to pay back

because there is not enough money to do so, thus causing the system to collapse

26. Because the government borrows money instead of creating it at no cost, it has to tax future income to pay its debt service to the financial class. This tax is an expense adding to the break-even cost of doing business and increases taxes to the populace

27. What stops the bank-led financial system from expanding credit and money without limit, including to their owned investment banking side? The obvious answer would be that it would stop when participants ran out of profitable opportunities. But this is not a convincing answer if the activities of the hyperactive intermediaries in aggregate create the perceived opportunities: credit growth breeds asset price bubbles that in turn breed credit growth. What stops it, is a crisis or collapse of the market used for collateral such as the 2008 mortgage crisis

28. Banks are profit-seeking, risk-taking financial institutions. One's money is at risk except for the insured amount. Therefore, they should not have the power to create money, but to only distribute it

29. Monetary reform will reduce the financialization of the American economic system. This means the economy is stimulated by the shift *from making things to the manipulation of money*, which involves: derivatives, mergers and acquisitions, venture capitalism, leverage buyouts, workouts and turnarounds, currency speculation, and arbitrage. One of the reasons for this excess is the creation power attached to the banking sector. The monetary system becomes the servant and not the master of the economy, as it is now!

30. Permanent increases in the money supply only come when there is a write down or total failure to repay a bank loan. Is bankruptcy an appropriate way of having permanent money for our economy? Of course not!

We believe we have listed more than enough reasons, *over two dozen*, to support the elimination of money creation by commercial bank lending. We need to create a transparent monetary creation system based on volume in circulation and inflation statistics with multiple delivery systems. The proposed system is *created to handle human errors*, which is not the current single banking system that is based on attaining human perfection through regulations.

If you do not get a clear understanding and you are not persuaded by my reasoning, you can do further reading and research. Therefore, to assist you further in your education and comprehension, I have prepared an extensive list of website addresses and books to read below.

RESEARCH & EVIDENCE for TRUE MONETARY REFORM

This issue *is so macro economically important and opaque* that I have listed books and other research below to provide *evidence* that **monetary reform that ends debt-created money** is **an absolute necessity**! I have listed them in order of importance:

The Lost Science of Money by Stephen Zarlenga – **This book is the ultimate in the global history and definition of money.** It has far more historical content than my book. The educational nonprofit of the American Monetary Institute (AMI) is at www.monetary.org. You can also attend the annual educational conference for extensive input!

The Bubble and Beyond by Michael Hudson – **This book has the best description and proof that the debt creating money systems are unsustainable.** His current book *Killing the Host: How Financial Parasites and Debt Destroy the Global Economy* is a summary of the former book with a description of the Great Recession and the U.S. bailout of the banks.

Sovereign Money, Beyond Reserve Banking by Joseph Huber— **This is for all academics and economists who are interested in researching monetary reform. His website is: www.sovereignmoney.eu.**

Secrets of the Temple by William Greider – **This book is the best and easiest to read when it comes to providing a description of the U.S. monetary history up to 1983. At the same time, he teaches you how this current system works.**

The Chicago Plan Revisited by Michael Kumhof – Depicts a model of monetary reform that can be successfully implemented without excess inflation.

Where Does Money Come From? by Josh Ryan-Collins, Tony Greenham, Richard Werner, and Andrew Jackson.

Metric for Money, Healthy Money, Citizen Owned Money Supply, and *The Root of U.S. Public & Private Debt.* These are pamphlets written by Professor Bob Blain, Ph.D. They give a very quick read on the definition, history, and alternatives for "debt" money.

Modernizing Money, by Andrew Jackson & Ben Dyson —**this is a wonderful descriptive book on the UK money system, with many creative ideas for reform. Their nonprofit: Positive Money can be found at** www.positivemoney.uk.

Free Money—Plan for Prosperity, by Rodger Malcolm Mitchell — **this book gives an excellent description of what our so-called National Debt really is.**

The Shifts and the Shocks, by Martin Wolf – The first internationally known financial writer who is considering embracing true monetary reform.

Web of Debt by Ellen Hodgson Brown – This is an excellent and easy read to help readers understand our current monetary system. But, it provides an incomplete solution to help our economies through public banking.

Between Debt and the Devil by Adair Turner – The most recent book on monetary reform; however, he recommends keeping a partial reserve banking system. This is still *unsustainable*!

We Hold These Truths – The Hope of Monetary Reform by Richard C. Cook

Rights vs. Privileges by Robert De Fremery

Fantopian by James Gibb Stuart – This is an excellent analogy explaining our monetary system using a historical setting.

Two Faces of Money by Geraldine Perry and Ken Fousek

The Secrets of the Federal Reserve by Eustace Mullins. This book is over the top. It should be read last in your research.

Coined by Kabir Sehal and *Biography of the Dollar* by Craig Karmin. These provide an easier and shorter history of the dollar—money. They offer no solutions.

MONETARY QUOTES from the FAMOUS

Benjamin Franklin—(From His Autobiography)

In one year, the conditions [of the Colonels] were so reversed that the era of prosperity ended, and a depression set in, to such an extent that the streets of the Colonies were filled with the unemployed... The colonies would gladly have borne the little tax on tea and other matters had it not been that England took away from the colonies their money, which created unemployment and dissatisfaction (Currency Act of 1764). **The inability of the colonists to get power to issue their own money permanently out of the hands of George III and the international bankers was the PRIME reason for the Revolutionary War.**

"The utility of this currency became, by time and experience, so evident as never afterwards to be disputed...increasing trade, building, and all the time increasing inhabitants though I now think there are limits beyond which the quantity may be hurtful."

President James Garfield

Whoever controls the volume of money in any country is absolute master of all industry and commerce... And when you realize that the entire system is easily controlled, one way or another, by a few powerful men at the top, you will not have to be told how periods of inflation and depression originate.

Horace Greeley—(about the Coinage Act of 1873)

We have stricken the shackles from four million human beings and brought all laborers to a common level, not so much by the elevation of the former slaves as by practically reducing the whole working population, white and black to a condition of serfdom. While boasting of our noble deeds, we are careful to conceal the ugly fact that by our iniquitous money system, we have nationalized a system of oppression which, though more refined, is not less cruel than the old system of chattel slavery.

President Abraham Lincoln

Abstract of Lincoln's Monetary Policy

Library of Congress

No. 23, 76th Congress, 1st Session, page 91. 1865

1. *Money is the creature of law, and the creation of the original issue of money should be maintained as the exclusive monopoly of national government. Money possesses no value to the state other than that given to it by circulation*

2. *Capital has its proper place and is entitled to every protection. The wages of men should be recognized in the structure of and in the social order as more important than the wages of money [interest]*

3. *No duty is more imperative for the government than the duty it owes the people to furnish them with a sound and uniform currency, and of regulating the circulation of the medium of exchange so that labor will be protected from a vicious currency [private bank-created, interest-bearing debt], and commerce will be facilitated by cheap and safe exchanges*

4. *The available supply of gold and silver being wholly inadequate to permit the issuance of coins of intrinsic value or paper currency convertible into coin of intrinsic value or paper currency convertible into coin in the volume required to serve the needs of the People, some other basis for the issue of currency must be developed, and some means other than that of convertibility into coin must be developed to prevent undue fluctuation in the value of paper currency or any other substitute for money intrinsic value that may come into use*

5. *The monetary needs of increasing numbers of people advancing towards higher standards of living can*

and should be met by the government. Such needs can be met by the issue of national currency and credit through the operation of a national banking system [or designated monetary authority]. The circulation of a medium of exchange issued and backed by the government can be properly regulated and redundancy of issue avoided by withdrawing from circulation such amounts as may be necessary by taxation, redeposit and otherwise. Government has the power to regulate the currency and credit of the nation

6. *Government should stand behind its currency and credit and the bank deposits of the nation. No individual should suffer a loss of money through depreciation or inflated currency of bank bankruptcy*

7. *Government, possessing the power to create and issue currency and credit as money and enjoying the right to withdraw both currency and credit from circulation by taxation and otherwise, need not and should not borrow capital at interest as a means of financing government work and public enterprise. The government should create issue and circulate all the currency and credit needed to satisfy the spending power of the government and the buying power of the consumers. The privilege of creating and issuing money is not only the supreme prerogative of government, but it is the government's greatest creative opportunity.*

8. *By adoption of these principles, the long-felt want for a uniform medium will be satisfied. The taxpayers will be saved immense sums of interest, discounts, and exchanges. The financing of all public enterprises, the maintenance of stable government and ordered progress, and the conduct*

of the Treasury will become matters of practical
administration. The people can and will be
furnished with a currency as safe as their own
government. Money will cease to be master and
become the servant of humanity. Democracy will
rise superior to the money power.

William Jennings Bryan

Excerpt from "Cross of Gold" Speech

The money problem facing the country from 1789 to
1896 existed because Congress never exercised its
authority to "coin money or regulate the value thereof"
– but rather delegated that authority, sometimes by
charter and sometimes by default, to the banking system.
This despite the provision in the Constitution that
charged Congress with the power to "coin money,
regulate the value thereof, and of foreign Coin, and fix
the Standards of Weight and Measures."

Congressman Charles A. Lindberg (Sr.)

From His Book, *Banking and Currency and The Money Trust*

Creating money out of commodities like gold and silver
and legislating value into them by making them legal
tender is the worst possible policy and the greatest
limitation placed upon advancing civilization. It would
be the same principle, though not in degree, as would be
the printing and giving of legal tender paper money by
the government to persons who give no consideration in
return. Neither gold nor any other metal or commodity
should be stamped with a value and made a legal tender.
Commodities may properly be stamped with their quality

and weight so that stamp may be used as exchange in commerce on their own merits. Neither person nor property is entitled to any specially conferred government privileges. To coin metal and make it legal tender gives a special value to metal which enables those possessing it to take undue advantage of the rest of us... If gold is worth all they claim for it, it needs no extra function. If, on the other hand, it is not able to retain its present relative value without being legal tender, then that is positive proof that it should not be legal tender. In the one case it is unnecessary; in the other case it is unjust.

Other Quotes by Lindberg

Those not favorable to the money trust could be squeezed out of business and the people frightened into demanding changes in the banking and currency laws, which the Money Trust would frame.

The government prosecuted other trusts, but supports the money trusts.

Henry Ford

"It is well that the people of the nation do not understand our banking and monetary system. For if they did, I believe there would be a revolution before tomorrow morning."

Robert B. Andersen

Secretary of Treasury under Dwight D. Eisenhower

"When a bank makes a loan it simply adds to the borrowers' deposit account in the bank by the amount of the loan. The money is not taken from anyone else's

deposit; it was not previously paid in the bank by anyone. It's new money, created by the bank for the use of the borrower."

Stephen Zarlenga

Director American Monetary Institute

"Over time, whoever controls the money system, controls the nation."

Chapter 10

SOLUTIONS

A completely new separate system for money creation with the incorporation of many "new money" delivery systems is the solution to reducing the first major flaw of capitalism. This reform is by far the most important economic decision to be made. To help you do your own historical research, we have narrowed down our recommended resources to four major books: *The Lost Science of Money* by Stephen Zarlenga, *The Bubble & Beyond* or *Killing the Host* by Michael Hudson, *The Secrets of the Temple* by William Greider, and *Sovereign Money, Beyond Reserve Banking* by Joseph Huber (recommended for academics and economists). Additional web resources include: www.monetary.org, www.soverignmoney.eu, and www.postivemoney.uk.

Taking into account the many failures of private and central banking over the centuries, we have come to the conclusion that it is necessary to eliminate both the private fractional reserve system of monetary creation from the commercial banking system and the interest charges on the national debt. We stand with President Jefferson and President Lincoln and insist that monetary creation belongs in government, not private banks. Benjamin Franklin, and Presidents Madison, Jackson, and Wilson joined Jefferson and Lincoln in that belief.

People are not perfect in practice or theory; therefore, delivery systems have to be diversified to reduce the severity of wrong decisions. The money creation power has to be placed back into a democratically elected government with checks and balances. Whoever controls the money controls the society. "Give me control of a nation's money supply, and I care not who makes its laws." That is a quote from Mayer Amschel Rothschild, the financier who started the Rothschild banking empire.

There are two major economic functions of a federal government. One is tax and spend (fiscal policy). The other is the creation and distribution of new money (monetary policy) which was written into the Constitution by our Founding Fathers as part of a compromise with the individual States. **It is in Article I, Section 8, and Clause 5 of the Constitution. Where it states: "To coin money, regulate the value thereof, and of foreign coin, and fix the standard of weights and measures."** "To coin" is a verb, meaning *make or create*. Congress licensed this power to the Federal Reserve in 1913. What they giveth, they can taketh away!

How New Money Should Be Created and Distributed

Money should be created by a federal **centralized** governmental process with as many checks and balances as possible. It *should not be a private process*! It is much too powerful to be in private hands with all the benefits going to a mere few in only one sector of an economy. Money is created by law and by allowing taxes and government usage fees to be paid by its currency, it creates a basis for legitimacy and acceptance by the population. **This creation process has to allow maximum dispersion by setting the total amount of new money distributed through decentralized distribution channels. These amounts are calculated by various inflationary formulas and statistics as guidelines.** This means we should not use debt for creation of money, nor interest rates to control the creation. Additional monetary research can be found in *Towards a New Monetary Paradigm: A Quantity Theorem of Disaggregated Credit* by Richard Werner.

In the process of creating money we need to decide *who* has the power to determine *how much is created*, and *where it will go*. There can be three operating alternatives within a government: executive branch, legislative branch, or a new separate entity. We don't care which of these is chosen, because people with built-in biases, beliefs, and political influences operate all of them. **We are more concerned with implementing monetary reform rather than who is running it.** In fact, we would like to see variations in operations among different governments to determine the best practice. (We will discuss specifics in Chapter 13.)

We believe there are three basic overall processes, whereby creating money can be effectively structured within a government, including an independent authority:

1. **Use monetary creation to fund government spending that is not funded by taxes (deficits). This would allow an increase in spending until the inflationary guidelines are met. This is the process recommended by the American Monetary Institute. It was submitted to Congress under the "Need Act" in 2010. It uses a separate monetary authority to create money and is distributed by the various spending alternatives passed by Congress, including paying of the student debt and giving the states 25% of the money created for their spending.**

2. **Use the current fiscal system (tax and spend) to fund programs that do not have an actual investment return (interest or capital gains) to the Treasury. Then use the monetary system to fund programs that have some type of return to the Treasury, using debt and stock instruments. See Chapter 13. It is a more diversified system that uses private companies for some of its distribution. It will be a more difficult system to manage, but it will provide more new money for the many needed projects without excess inflation. This alternative should be more politically acceptable to the right.**

3. **We eliminate the fiscal (tax and spend) system all together and have only a monetary system. The legislative body makes spending decisions and funds it only by creating money. It then creates a progressive taxing system to reduce the money supply to control excess or hyperinflation. This is similar to No. 1 above.**

The following is a list of potential distribution systems. A majority of these systems *should be in private hands* with the government providing the amount of new money, operational oversight, and the regulatory guidelines for their operations. They will use direct currency issue, equity- stock and debt vehicles to deliver the new money. **These are NOT creation systems, but distribution systems**. We call them banks, for the lack of a better term. We will discuss each of these potential distribution systems in some detail in Chapter 13.

1. Government spending into circulation-Paying the deficit with created money.
2. Primary Housing Bank
3. Environmental Bank
4. Venture Capital Bank
5. Land and Infrastructure Bank
6. Community and SBA Bank
7. Student Loan Bank
8. Microfinance Bank
9. Nonprofit and Cultural Bank
10. Agriculture Bank
11. Commercial Banking & Pension Assistance
12. Local Governments and Public Banking
13. Food Stamp Bank

Increasing the type of distribution instruments to distribute new money

Where is it written that new money is distributed *only by debt*, i.e., loans? By the way we cling to our old, antiquated system, you would think using debt to create and distribute new money was one of the Ten Commandments! There is no reason why we can't establish *private institutions* to distribute new money through investments of **equity (common stock), lending of debt (loans)**, and a **combination of equity and debt**, along with **direct government spending**. The reason we should have debt and equity distribution vehicles rather than all direct government spending is because this process of having some government investment return reduces the monetary supply as it is paid to the Treasury. This is the same way that paying Federal taxes reduces the money supply in circulation. All loans and equity investments will have the proper underwriting and due diligence for placement. These additional instruments of distribution reduce the chances of excess inflation by having a payback to the Treasury, thus allowing more new money for programs and projects to be created and distributed depending on the inflationary environment.

There is precedence to using **equity** as a distribution vehicle for newly created money. Islamic banking, for example, provides equity return *rather than just interest return*. Because of religious beliefs, a mutual risk and a goal of non-clashing interests, Islamic banks developed a system of shared risk banking. There is a less adversarial relationship between lenders and borrowers. Actually, our big banks and insurance companies currently make these types of participation loans to large commercial real estate projects. An equity-based new money system still yields return to the Treasury and it may be a greater return, but it occurs at the time of sale, gifting or refinancing.

In an effective monetary program, in order to reduce the extreme negative effects of interest rate fluctuations and the reluctance of private enterprises to invest, especially in economic down turns and extreme uncertainty, new money **equity instruments** become an absolute necessity. See Chapter 13 under Venture Capital Bank. This equity distribution process also increases long term investing rather than short term returns (See Section IV).

Many positive things happen when there is less debt service (interest charges): Business survival is heightened, competition increases, production is improved. There is more economic stability, and consequently prices of goods and services are kept lower. This also allows for more monetary expansion without excess inflation. There is less displacement of employers and employees. Even when interest rates rise, industries will continue to grow. The housing industry usually first hit by rising interest rates, i.e. subprime, will stay healthier. When mortgage payments are lowered by **equity ownership** returns, more folks can get into and stay in their homes, which mean fewer foreclosures. Also, business survival is heightened by lower loan payments, thus fewer bankruptcies. This causes substantially less strain on the entire financial system. (Interest rates do not control the money supply under monetary reform. Therefore, there are no rising interest rates on short-term notes to unbelievable heights, causing a severe downturn, like the early 1980's.)

These recommended systems are for the first use of created money; they do NOT replace the current private financial system which is the sequential use of created "old money"! They actually expand this system by providing more capital and opportunities for individuals and businesses to participate. A safe, diversified, and stable money system provides a less volatile foundation for the financial markets.

Chapter 11

AVOIDING EXCESS INFLATION & OPERATIONS

As we have seen over the centuries, the power to create money left in private hands has been devastating. It is now time to return it back to democratic governments with checks and balances, **keeping in mind there is an unlimited demand for money. It should not be a zero-sum game only benefiting the banking sector.**

The first task is for Congress to take back this power, which is very similar to the power of the purse strings—*spending*. Move the Federal Reserve into the Treasury Department to continue to regulate the commercial banks. The Treasury should then start paying off the national debt as it matures, with 0% Treasuries or plain money. This will eliminate the interest on the national debt, a significant part of the budget, or deficit.

Treasuries are basically used for investing and would not be spent causing any significant spike in inflation. A significant portion is already in and will stay as reserves in other countries, including our own Social Security Trust Fund. Some of the money, mostly from investors, will be looking for a new investment with some rate of return and safety which will help the financial service industry and the insured deposits in commercial banks.

This is a Win-Win for the commercial banks. With the elimination or substantial reduction in new Treasuries issued, the first-place investors will look is the FDIC insured deposits in our banks, which become pure intermediaries. These savings accounts will be the new Treasuries. Therefore, they should be directly backed by the government; not by an agency like the FDIC which only *implies* total government backing. **This will easily fund the commercial banks for their continued operations. They will compete for deposits, which will give higher pay outs (with a cap) to the savers. It will also be much less volatile than the current**

banking model. Banks will be allowed to invest these funds in diversified portfolios with guidelines set up by the regulators. All, I mean *all* investment and savings vehicles have principle risk except Treasuries and insured savings accounts. They do have inflation risk! The only thing that lowers principle risk is a diversified portfolio, which can have inflation protection.

Commercial banking will convert to intermediaries (like a mutual fund) which will also make the banking system safer from collapse and individual bankruptcies. The conversion should reduce regulations, and the banks will retain and increase their distribution operations from the new avenues of distribution listed and described in Chapter 13. **They will still make a lot of money! It is a Win-Win!**

Other investors will move to the financial services industry with their extensive array of investment vehicles, some owned by the commercial banks. Thus, we will still maintain a very active private financial system. Also, if we continue to promote competition and productivity, this reduces inflationary pressures and allows for more issuance of money. If you want more information on the banking transition and answering other objections, you should read Chapter five of *Creating New Money* by Huber & Robertson of the New Economics Foundation, and Chapter eight of *Modernizing Money*, by Jackson and Dyson. There are also others that have modeled and answered this transition question.

Since the process of creating money has an immense amount of power, the next task is to create new money with as little concentration of influence and corruption as possible. (See Chapter 12) We also need to create a government structure to reduce the possibility of excess or hyperinflation.

Hopefully, most of you will agree that an increased number of distribution systems (many in private hands), along with a government creation system with checks and balances will allow for an adequate monetary system. This system can be created for the 21st Century modern economy without excess inflation, a system that is diversified in order to reduce the consequences of human error!

For the economists who like numbers and econometrics, please review the website of Professor Karoru Yamaguchi of the University of Doshisha in Kyoto, Japan at http://www.muratopia.org/index.html. He has created a system dynamics model that substantiates this evolutionary change. The current system is a failure in systems design and he has written a new book, *Public Banking*, which is a model for monetary reform for the Japanese system.

Summary of the Elimination of Excess/Hyperinflation & Asset Bubbles

Since the only objection, perceived or real, that anyone can give you for monetary reform is that of *excess inflation*, we decided to summarize the many reasons why our recommended reforms will not cause excess inflation or asset bubbles. These reasons are in the body of the text. But, remember, in the last 100 years, most hyperinflationary environments had a central bank present! Most were caused by a severe balance of payment deficits collapsing exchange rates, thereby raising import prices and, hence, domestic prices. Never in modern history has hyperinflation resulted from governments monetizing domestic debt. *It has been caused by foreign debt service collapsing the exchange rate*. See Michael Hudson's *The Bubble and Beyond.*

Moderate inflation is good, and excess inflation is bad. Growth and wages are not significant factors in causing excess inflation in the overall economy. The economic boom in the 1990's proved this. The major factor that creates excess inflation is too much money issued and put into circulation by the banking system. The Federal Reserve monetizes too much debt created by deficit spending, while chasing an inadequate supply of goods and services and/or indiscriminate subsidies. The cost of fossil fuels is also a current significant factor because it permeates through the entire economy as a major cost variable. The following is a list of protocols to implement to keep excess inflation in check:

1. Diversity of monetary delivery systems. This especially helps in avoiding asset bubbles and allows for more monetary expansion. Gradual implementation of any new distribution system helps in reducing inflation and currency crisis
2. Encourage production and productivity. We now live in an "abundance world". The private sector is extremely productive and can produce most of the goods and services We have excess capacity for most goods and services, which is a deflationary factor—we just don't have enough quality consumers. The expansion and diversity of the monetary functions will aid in this production and competition
3. Reduction of high interest rate charges, which is a cost of doing business and places an upward pressure on prices. Businesses that cannot afford or are not allowed to borrow decrease production, reducing supply relative to demand, driving up prices
4. **Encouraging savings and investing rather than over consumption of goods.** Reducing the strain on natural, nonrenewable resources
5. **Encouraging spending on personal services rather than over spending on goods.** Also, reducing the strain on natural, nonrenewable resources
6. Having the Commerce Department continue to create and publish, for transparency, an array of inflation statistics from many formulas based on asset prices, goods and services with, and without the price of oil
7. Having many checks and balances in the creation and distribution of money in the Federal Government. (President, Treasury, Judiciary, Commerce, Senate, House.) The debate will be how much and where to increase or decrease monetary creation based on the inflationary statistics instead of this

philosophical debate. (See Chapter 12)

8. Voters will be able to cast their votes based on inflationary management of the country
9. Currency markets should be monitored in the long term to help control any excess inflation
10. **Increasing taxation removes money from the system**
11. Competition usually keeps upward spirals of prices in check. Increasing antitrust enforcement and/or regulating monopolies and oligopolies helps. (See Section III)
12. Substantially encourage **the 5Rs: Reuse, Repair, Renewable, Regeneration and Recycling** to reduce the demand pressures on raw materials—commodities and on the environment
13. Elimination of "fractional reserve banking". This current system creates money by making loans. However, it doesn't create the interest to pay for the loans, which can't get paid—unless there is a continuous supply of new money. This forces new loans, causing inflationary conditions and guaranteed financial collapse
14. Trade deficits can be very detrimental to the value of a country's currency. The U.S. has less risk than other countries, as they are the major reserve and trading currency of the world
15. Selling Treasury bonds—zero coupons—will decrease the money supply. This operation will be substantially curtailed, but retained for emergency spending needs

Inflation should be at least 2%, as anything lower is too close to human error, bringing deflation, causing recession/depression and severe human hardship. The declining value of money (inflation) is factored in the decision making of businesses and individuals. *Stability of this lower rate is the key!*

Summary of Monetary Solutions

1. Pay off all U.S. Treasuries as they mature with Zero Coupon Treasuries or just money

2. Eliminate "Fractional Reserve Banking" by making them direct financial intermediaries but retaining FDIC type insurance and distribution functions, creating a Win-Win scenario
3. Move the Federal Reserve into the Treasury for bank regulation, making it a real Federal agency!
4. Increase the number of new money distribution systems from 2 to 13
5. Use direct currency issue for some of our government spending
6. Use equity as well as debt instruments as distribution vehicles for new money
7. Make the creation of money as a power of a transparent democracy with many checks and balances, using a separate monetary authority or the legislature
8. Enforce anti-trust regulation in the commercial banking industry (See Section III)
9. **Introduce excess inflationary protocols**
10. We need to separate the operational processes of creation and distribution of new money

The world needs capital to fund, expand, explore, invest, research, clean up the environment, conserve fresh water, and to create goods and services cleanly and efficiently. Private capital (old money) cannot do it alone. The private monetary system was the cause of the current crisis. The answer to funding the future is *monetary reform, not to debate tax and spend as usual.* **By providing our nation with a medium of exchange that truly reflects the productive and consumptive capacity of our own citizens—rather than burdening us with unsustainable debt in order to get currency into circulation—we can become a truly independent country.** We would be able to preserve our natural resources, invest in needed infrastructure, create a business boom and adequately reward our citizens. In addition, we would no longer need to mortgage third world countries—or ourselves—in order to support our growing "so-called" debt. As we have seen over the centuries, the power to create money in private hands has been devastating. It is now time to turn it back to democratic governments *with checks and balances* and create a 21st Century Win-Win Economy.

Chapter 12

NEW METHODS OF MONEY CREATION – NOT DISTRIBUTION

The creation of money has been primarily in *private* hands through the creation of debt. I feel it is too powerful of a process with unlimited demand to primarily benefit private owners. Therefore, the process should be exclusively in governments' hands with transparency and many checks and balances. The monetary reform movement's major recommendation is to create a separate **monetary authority**. I will review this recommendation and discuss leaving it in a democratic legislature, because *it is very similar to current spending decisions.* Keep in mind that *deficit spending* eventually forces *monetary creation.* Monetary reform is such an important issue that I will accept either! **It is far more important to have a correct system without debt creation rather than focusing on *who* is running the system.**

There are several recommendations for the formation of a new government agency, or agencies, to handle the creation and distribution of new money. Many feel that there would be less self-interest decision-making in a separate monetary authority. I agree. But, this group would still be made up of people with their own conflicts, biases, obligations, and political influences. Also, a self-contained committee will have less transparency than an open legislature. You have to then answer the major questions: What branch does it fall under; executive, legislative, or a new branch? Who appoints them and confirms them? What is their term? What is the party make up of this agency? Will the President and/or legislature have veto power? One can see a whole new set of conflicts and politics. It will definitely be more difficult to establish a new one than to keep an already operating legislature.

The big question is: Will a legislature pass monetary reform that gives this power to another political body? I doubt it! They did it once in the 1913 Federal Reserve Act. They probably learned their lesson! But, the political right might like this separate monetary authority. The banks have used this bogus separation issue to retain this monetary power. In the United States, there is no historical evidence to back them up. In fact, it is the opposite with the successful Colonial Currency, Continental Currency, and the Civil War currency—Greenbacks.

The current major political arguments are basically on macroeconomic philosophy (and power), not on operations. **The debate should only be on how much and where to spend, tax, and create money, *not* on philosophy.** It should be debated, argued, and fought over! It should be more civil than arguing over macroeconomic philosophy. These decisions should be in the political arena for voters to decide who is making the correct decisions and managing the country without excess inflation or recessions.

The next task is to create a government system under the current structure with many checks and balances. This system would create and distribute new money with as little concentration of influence and corruption that the power of creating money brings with it. There should also be government protocols to reduce the possibility of excess or hyperinflation.

Since spending bills start in the House of Representatives, so should money creation, which is very similar. There are two things the House should do: First, establish with regulations and oversight the various distribution banking systems. The second is to annually determine how much new money is issued and distributed in each distribution system.

Checks and Balances

The House needs to set up a new, major committee labeled, the **Monetary Committee**—whose main function would be to determine how much money to issue each year. There should be a subcommittee set up for each distribution banking system recommending how much should be allocated to each system. The deficit subcommittee would be in charge of determining how much to create or borrow to cover any deficit. Remember, new money creation eliminates the deficit. The subcommittee budgets would be approved by the overall Monetary

Committee of the House, followed by the process of **House approval, Senate approval**, and then the **President's signature or veto**. This provides the first set of checks and balances.

The Treasury Dept. will operate the government distribution systems and oversee the private banks (distribution systems). This will provide another check and balance. **There will be a monetary computer in the Treasury Department that creates and sends out the digital money approved by the Congress and the President, and provides allocation information for their decision-making.** The Defense Department along with the Treasury should protect the "Monetary Creation Computer". We have learned from the past that counterfeiting can lead to a major destruction of the currency (Revolutionary War).

The Commerce Department will continue and expand its inflationary formulas and statistics to cover geographical regions, industries, and asset bubbles; plus monitor the currency, gold, and other commodity markets. They will also make it completely transparent and provide public access through the Internet. This will help guide our representatives to avoid excess inflation. It will also provide public awareness *so that the election process becomes another check and balance.*

The Justice Department will also set up a monetary inspector general to make sure the rules and regulations are followed in the creation and distribution of new money, both in the private and public sector. This is another check and balance.

This will be the basic flow of creating new money in the United States while avoiding a creation of a new monetary authority or another branch of government. *What is important is that it is not just spending money into circulation, but also loaning and investing money into the economy.* Loaning and investing will allow for more new money to flow into the economy without excess inflation because there will be an annual reduction in the money in circulation from loan payments and investment returns.

Chapter 13

MONETARY DISTRIBUTION OPERATIONS

The following is a brief description of various distribution systems for "new money" only. Some of these systems are new while others are changed to adjust for the creation of money without using debt. New firms do not have to be established; existing firms (like banks, credit unions, and other loan brokers) would take on a majority of these operations.

Government spending into circulation: The basic monetary reform movement's proposal is to have a monetary authority issue new money either to pay for the deficits or to fund additional programs. This is labeled "spending into circulation". This process is simpler to manage than having a substantial number of different distribution systems. Spending into circulation will work but it has its limits in distribution diversity. I believe we need an even larger variety of distribution to create a more vibrant economy and to encourage bipartisan support.

Family Housing Bank: This system will consolidate all the current Federal Housing Agencies (Fannie Mae, Freddie Mac, etc.) into one monetary system for **home loans in first position on primary residences** up to a maximum amount similar to the FHA limit. Currently 65-80% of new home first mortgages are guaranteed by the U.S. government that protects investors from risk of default. This agency will provide a variety of low interest rates (1-4%), long-term mortgages (30-40 years) for qualified individuals throughout the country. The only restriction will be the annual geographical allotment by a city or area to avoid another housing bubble. Underwriting, distribution, and administration of these mortgages will be handled by the current private mortgage brokerage and service industry. **All loans are still underwritten properly.** The borrower still has to have the ability to pay it! Additionally, 50 year mortgages at 1% for low income housing apartments should be part of this distribution system. This is similar to the current Section 8 HUD programs. All other real estate loans (residential and nonresidential), like second mortgages, will be "old money" issued by the commercial banking system and private mortgage market.

Environmental Bank: This channel is probably the most important new distribution system. **The major reason that new environmental technologies have not been implemented by businesses and individuals is lack of low cost capital.** Instead of providing tax credits and other tax incentives *(affecting fiscal budgets)* for this retooling, the monetary authorities can provide very low cost, long term, no down payment loans for this equipment. These loans do not start repayment until 30 days after the technology is operational. This provides a much greater incentive for owners to purchase this equipment as there is no initial out of pocket cost, plus, the payment would be substantially less than the savings the new technology will provide. This system could be only governmental, but I see no reason that private loan brokers and commercial bankers could not be heavily involved in underwriting and servicing these loans.

Example 1: A large industrial building owner wants to install solar units on a roof. This bank would loan him a Length of the Equipment loan of 30 years at 1%. A $100,000 loan would only be $377 per month. This would be substantially lower than the savings to the power company, leaving room for maintenance and profit. Then, the building owner could sell any extra-generated power that was not used. There would be a line around the block to get these loans. Therefore, you would need to limit the total quantity of loans in a geographic area so there would be no price gouging or control prices on the installers and manufacturers. (Currently, there is a glut of solar equipment from lack of sales.)

Example 2: There are many areas around the globe with severe water shortages that are still using regular irrigation and not micro-drip irrigation. This is low-tech conservation, and the same loan can be acquired to install these systems. Again, the savings on their water bill will cover the loan payment and maintenance as well as provide a profit; therefore, every farmer, large and small, will be in line for this loan.

This distribution system is how we can afford to convert the world from fossil fuels to non- polluting renewable fuels, while cleaning up our polluted oceans and land, and other environmental projects. It is almost self-motivating because of the low cost of loans, but some regulation to require conversion over time will probably be necessary.

Venture Capital Bank: This bank can be created to provide new money to industries and in those regions that need investment capital. Instead of distributing these funds using debt with current, ongoing payments (debt service), **this system would use equity (stock) as a return.** The monetary authority would create the money and mostly private firms would do the distribution. This non-long-term government equity position would be non-controlling and nonvoting in commercial operations. (We do not want any hint of socialism.) The government would receive its return upon sale, liquidation, dividends, or refinancing. This nonvoting stock can be managed similarly to standard portfolio management. If the stock is public, sales of this equity must be managed without substantial price fluctuations of all the stock coming to market at once. If the stock is private, the stock would be held until its sale, liquidation, or when it goes public. There is enough brainpower on Wall Street to assist the government with any public stock sale decisions, but most of the nonpublic stock that is not liquid cannot be sold by the government. The private investment managers would handle this decision-making process. For example, Israel has a sovereign investment fund that receives an equity return. This is not unlike the current U.S. Small Business Innovation Research Program (SBIR) and Defense Department agencies that currently provide billions in only loans and grants to high-risk companies at a much earlier stage of development than do most private venture capital firms. (See "The Entrepreneurial State" by Marianna Mazzucato.) We just need equity investing on the monetary side where we can have some return to the Treasury in the form of stock dividends, capital gains and possibly royalty income from licensing contracts. Some may argue that the government already receives a return on its investments through taxing corporate profits, but many firms have lowered their real returns by tax shelters and havens—offshore. (See Corporate Tax in Chapter 23).

This equity process can operate in three different ways:

1. We currently have a successful private venture capital industry. The monetary authority could create money and invest with these venture capitalists with a matching program that has the same terms as their other investors. It would be voluntary for the venture capital firm that would license with the monetary authority. There would be cherry picking regulations to protect the government. It would require an equal investment in all ventures. In boom times, it would probably only be necessary to match 10%+ of other funds raised. In down times, like 2008, it could go to 90% to help stimulate the economy. The first thing that new firms will do once they get funded is hire new employees. Also, there could be some ***general*** direction of allocation, or the amounts of matching funds, by the monetary authority to specific industries, geographical regions, and environmental companies that are deemed necessary.

2. The monetary authority could create a whole array of private investment firms that would directly provide new equity capital for needed areas and deserving companies. They could coordinate with other sources of debt funding, i.e., commercial and community banks, and SBA loans to provide 100% of a funding source.

3. The government could have its own internal allocation system that could fund direct equity capital to large and small firms in needy areas and/or environmental projects. A pure government agency does not need to have a quick turnaround or profit. It only has to keep excess inflation under control by limiting amounts and reducing defaults.

Examples: A Fortune 1000 company is considering a facility. If the company places it in an area of the country that needs employment, the monetary authority invests 10%-50% of the capital requirements for the facility. In return, it receives nonvoting equity, such as stock options. It would be management's choice, but it would certainly be an attractive option to use its own capital or pay debt service on a loan.

Another example allocates capital to new and old businesses in blight areas. If the owner is qualified, has an effective business plan, and the business is needed, the infusion of money would provide immediate employment and services to the region. **The absence of interest and principle payments enhances the survival rate unlike the SBA and Community Bank debt financing.** Certainly this is a higher risk scenario, but there is a higher return upon sale, gifting, or refinancing. This equity financing can also be used in financing primary residences for needy families. Many families with successful employment histories cannot come up with the down payment or afford no or low down payment loans. This funding can provide down payments for qualified buyers. A return, again, comes from the sale, refinancing or gifting of the home. (There are similar programs in existence, but they are limited in scope.)

This venture capital equity distribution system represents a joint effort with the monetary authority and private capital venture capital firms, which mainly invests in private enterprises. The lack of cash flow drain enhances the chances of success. Of course, there will be allocation errors, but not to the extent that the current debt system has made throughout its existence. This system would be more diverse, provide for more competition, more employment and increase the variety of goods and services creating a healthy economic environment without excess inflation.

Special Note: Some people feel that the government is too heavily involved in this recommendation. I want to reiterate that this system

is mainly using private firms for distribution, similar to our banking structure, providing equity funding to only private enterprises.

Land and Infrastructure Bank: Land is **a non-wasting asset**. The government can create money to purchase land for any reason, including for the military, bridges, roads, schools, etc. This land purchase is held as **collateral** and can be sold well into the future, if not needed. An example would be the federal government purchasing land for a local school. It would lease this land to the school district for a dollar per year. When the school closes many decades in the future, the government sells the land at the going market price. This same system can also be used to purchase lands for national parks and preserves. In addition, the system can be used to sell some of its land holdings that are not needed. Buying the land for the government would increase the monetary supply, and selling government land would decrease the monetary supply. This would be solely a government operation using private real estate brokers.

This is how we can fund the repairs or replacements of our crumbling infrastructure. For those projects that have a toll charge for usage, we could use a very long-term, low interst loan, such as a 50+ year loan; otherwise it is straight spending by the governments. In other words if the government wanted to build a bridge that charges a toll it could use the toll revenue to pay for the building of the bridge. This type of funding will allow for quick repair of infrastructure.

The Community Bank and SBA: These loan systems should be expanded to include a wider variety of small and local businesses. These are job builders! Create them with a lower interest cost and longer amortizations to increase successes. They can also be participating (equity) loans to lower the cost of the debt service. This would remain mostly a private operation as it is now.

Student Loan Bank: I believe that all education from preschool through university should be basically free. But, on any student loans, there should be a maximum interest charge of 1% with long maturities. This would be a government operation delivered through the schools.

The current supply of student loans provides a perfect example of the lack of regulation and/or too much money going into one arena. **The increase in school tuitions far exceeds the other inflation rates except for healthcare.** In all the monetary delivery systems, we have to watch out for excessive price increases and bubbles. Currently we are graduating a lot of debt slaves that have little hope of quickly—or if *ever*—paying off their loans. This drastically hurts the main street economy, because this interest and principle is funneled into the financial sector. The Need Act pays off all student debt with newly created money.

Microfinance Bank: Most of these programs are funded through charitable donations. The monetary authorities could create additional new money to help fund these job creating and anti-poverty programs with substantially less interest charges and possibly an equity component. This distribution would be a private operation as it is now.

Agriculture Bank: Instead of providing substantial subsidies on the fiscal side, the government can provide more emergency loans and low or no cost long and short-term loans for small and organic farmers. The large corporate farmers have the girth to use the commercial banking system. Distribution operations could be the same as those being used today.

Nonprofit and Cultural Bank: This area should provide low cost loans with long maturities for nonprofits and cultural institutions (new and old) that have a revenue stream to repay. An example is funding the construction and ownership of a museum that charges admission to repay the loan. Because the maturity can be 40, 50, or 70 years, and the interest charge is low, the actual payment becomes so low that a fraction of the admission charge will repay the loan. This system will become one of the more important areas in the global economy. We are becoming extremely productive with machines and robots (See Section VI). This means we need fewer workers to produce all the goods and services the globe can consume. Innovation and service jobs will help, but will be nowhere close to employing the global working population.

This funding will provide those jobs that will be needed to continue to have enough quality customers and create a healthy 21st Century, Global Win-Win Economy. Special private loan brokers and commercial banks can handle the distribution.

Commercial Banking and Pension Assistance: The current commercial banking system of for-profit banks and non-profit banks should retain their insured deposit competitive advantage. In the absence of the need to issue Treasuries, these insured deposits will replace the Treasuries and cause a significant increase in deposits. Therefore, the current banking system would not need any allocation of new money. Nevertheless, there should be an emergency provision that allocates new money to the banks, if needed. This emergency feature could be made broader to include other finance service companies. **This retention of insured deposits is just as important to the many *depositors* as it is to the banks.** The banks would pay an unregulated, competitive interest (maybe a cap) and be allowed to invest in a regulated, substantially diversified portfolio backing these deposits. This would allow a majority of families to have a safe savings account with a reasonable return.

Under proper guidelines, created money can be used to assist unfunded pension plans both public and private. This is only a government operation. This solves the problem of pension underfunding by providing money that costs nothing to make as long as you watch for fraudulent behavior and of course excess inflation.

Local Governments: Any new money system needs to include local governments either in the form of a direct issuance or to be used to help fund local public banks (City, County, State and Postal Banks). North Dakota has the only public bank in the United States, although there are plenty of them in other countries. The North Dakota bank is 95+ years old and has been very successful. It is currently partially funded within the "fractional reserve system", which would be eliminated under monetary reform and replaced by direct grants by the federal government. In the management of this system, the authorities need to make sure there is not excessive local spending to prevent an asset bubble. **Also, the states and other local governments will have more flexibility in their taxation.** This occurs because of the reduction of Federal taxation, resulting from a new monetary creation and diversified distribution system funding many of the Federal programs and providing stimulus to the economy. **(The Need Act provides for 25% of the created money to go to the states for their decisions on spending!)**

Food Stamp Bank: Since food is a basic necessity for life and is currently paid for by a credit card, which is basically money, it can be paid for on the monetary side of government like a direct currency issue of new money.

Special Note on Digital Currencies like Bitcoin. These new online developments are really used as a different and competitive payment system or transfer agent clearinghouses, rather than banks. Remember, 97% of money is already digital. They were funded by investment and have a volatile pricing mechanism with a cap on the amount in the system. Therefore, they have very little, if any, money creation powers. What is important is the block chain technology used to manage and protect the system. The same should be used by governments in protecting the monetary-creating computer.

SECTION II

Not Enough Customers

"Employees are also Customers and Clients."

Chapter 14

GLOBAL UNEMPLOYMENT

There are over 200 million people unemployed in the world. This figure does not include the underemployed and underpaid. The latest Gallup Underemployment Index now stands at 19% of the global work force. Most economists only review and discuss the industrialized nations' unemployment, which does not count the over two billion who are only substance farmers and fishermen. Why is this happening?

The major reason is that the private sector's production of goods and services, including agriculture, is continuing its significant march on productivity. This productivity is a two-edged sword. Productivity reduces the number of employees and working hours. At the same time it makes products less expensive and increases the quantities available for distribution. We do not live in a world of scarcity anymore! In fact, most of our firms are not at full capacity. But, it reduces the number of employees who are the customers/clients/consumers. Innovation helps, but it will not increase employment enough to create a quality economy. Can you imagine if agriculture in India, Indonesia, and China becomes just a bit more productive? We will see millions more migrate to the cities looking for jobs that are not there.

In Europe we see "social dumping" where there are foreign workers under local labor standards. In the U.S. we have seen illegal immigration escalated by employers searching for lower labor costs. Because these labor costs are still too high we see many U.S. companies look to maximize their profits by moving jobs to lower paying countries. First to Mexico, then to China, Vietnam, and now to Laos and others; they are running out of countries! These low slave wages do not allow the workers to purchase enough of the goods and services that they produce. Paying people 71 cents an hour, as we did when we began to move to China, means that these employees can hardly purchase anything from their labor! No wonder China has extensive inventories and has to implement a trillion dollar stimulus to increase domestic spending. What has happened in the USA during layoffs, downsizing and low pay is that people start borrowing to spend and/or live by using payday loans, credit cards, and subprime mortgages. Of course, they cannot pay it back and eventually the financial system collapses as in 1929 and 2008. What are we going to do with all these people? Put them in jail or concentration camps? How about making them quality customers, clients, consumers and citizens? In the beginning of Richard Wolf's book, *Capitalism Hits the Fan*, there is an excellent description of the reasons for these macroeconomic failures.

Over the last 150 years, we have seen companies and whole economies crash because there are not enough quality customers and clients. The lack of customers has resulted in many business bankruptcies because of reduced sales. The reason that there is a lack of customers is because businesses treat labor and employees as a competitive marketplace under a microeconomic philosophy.

Chapter 15

EMPLOYEES ARE CONSUMERS

There are two basic fields of economics: *microeconomics* and *macroeconomics*. Micro is the study of individual markets and companies geared to making profits. Macro is the study of the whole economy. The objective of microeconomics is profit making. The objective of macroeconomics is to have a quality economy with a larger number of healthy and wealthy clients. The conflict arises when businesses start cutting labor costs in order to maximize profits—as they should—but as a result, the amount of sales decline because there are fewer customers or well paid customers. **The words "employee", "wages" and "labor" are micro terms. The words "customer", "client", and "consumer" are macro terms describing the same thing!**

Unfortunately, most business people think only on a microeconomic basis making a profit. They do not think about the macroeconomic basis that creates a lot of quality customers. The result is a lot of conflict, misinformation, and confusion. This is the reason why you see a lot of outsourcing, labor strife, and strikes around the world. One sees businessmen reducing the number of employees and always attempting to lower their wages and fringe benefits because it lowers the company's labor costs. The question is how far down do wages have to go before we get to slave labor and for owners to be happy? Neighboring businesses macroeconomics, will lose sales revenues, because their customers have been laid off or have had their salaries reduced. This microeconomic strategy fails to account for the macroeconomic consequences of losing customers or reducing their purchasing power.

The current solutions have been minimum wage regulations and labor unions. The real business solution is to eliminate competition based on living wages and fringe benefits. I am not talking about eliminating the competition in hiring employees that will be paid above the living wage.

Implementing this is easier said than done, and I will discuss the solution in the last section.

Owners want to pay employees as little as possible to increase their profits. This results in the creation of inadequate customers. To compensate for this effect, the government's domestic spending agenda helps underpaid workers by providing programs that they cannot afford to purchase, such as education, food stamps, medical and retirement benefits, etc. Labor unions, labor laws, minimum wages, and labor regulations offer assistance in overcoming this major problem in our world today. Perversely, it is usually these same conservative business owners who oppose these benefits! Instead, business owners should be concerned about their competition paying uncompetitive wages. This is unfair competition, because it hurts the overall economy. However, quality customers can be created by paying wages high enough to sustain and enhance every worker's ability to purchase quality goods and services. **Therefore, we should develop standards for a Quality Customer Minimum Wage instead of the present understanding and application of just a minimum wage. It is up to us capitalists' owners to take care of our customers, clients, and consumers.**

The argument is that the price of goods will substantially increase if wages are raised. The labor cost component is not the only component in the pricing mechanism. A reasonable increase in wages (fringe benefits) does not increase prices at the same rate. It is usually much smaller. Also, wages are deductible, so any increases are partially paid by reduced taxation. Therefore, prices can go up somewhat, but customer demand goes up also, creating more employment as well as a better economic and community environment. There are rising wages in the current capitalistic system, but not enough to create an adequate diverse consumer base. The world's production systems can produce (supply) enough for everyone, but the demand is not there because the people do not make enough to buy it or do not have enough money. This was basically the major cause of the great depression in the 1930's and the many other severe economic conditions that preceded it.

Therefore, minimum wage regulations must be based on geographical regions and age. The other argument is if the minimum wage is too high, employers will not hire younger employees as trainees, interns, or apprentices. The UK has solved this by having a lower minimum wage for the youngest in their work force. Of course, this is not as necessary today since this is the first time in history that the youngsters are teaching the older employers with their advanced computer skills and social media savvy.

Another argument against minimum wages is that increases in wages causes excess inflation. First, wages are only one part of the pricing decisions of managers. In manufacturing, only 20-30% of their costs are in wages. Therefore, a 50% increase in wage costs would only translate to a 10-15% one-time price increase. A 5% increase would only translate to a 1-1.5% price increase. This assumes that a business could pass the increase right through to customers. There are many other factors in pricing, like competition, cost of raw materials, energy costs, etc. These labor cost increases can also be absorbed by lowering profits.

Macroeconomic history has shown that minimum wages have sustained economies since their modern inception about 80 years ago. Every statistic I have seen proves this point. What is important to businesses is that their competition does not compete against them with significant differences in basic wages.

There should not be any significant competition within any industry based on hourly wages for the same job. This means there should not be any significant differences in hourly wages for the same job in a different state, county, city, or country. However, we should only see small differences in basic wages due to differences in costs of living throughout the world. Competition should be based on many other business factors, including labor utilization, pricing, marketing, and higher paid employees. Competition for labor, based solely on low wages, reduces the number of customers and their ability to buy more goods and services. In 1907, Henry Ford was the first to get this right, by almost doubling the daily wages of his workers so that they could buy his Model-T. The economists and businessmen of the era thought this was going to be an economic disaster. They were obviously wrong.

What currently hides this flaw creating the quality customer is consumer, debt such as credit cards, equity lines of credit, and the necessity for working spouses. The government has helped to abate this problem with substantial government employment. Another significant cause of the great depression was when the public had no access to credit because the Fed tightened monetary policy. Wages could not sustain the economy especially when there was no government spending safety net, and few government jobs.

In summary, we need quality customer minimum wage and protective wage differential tariffs to protect our customers and the economy from extremely low wage slave labor operations. As we raise wages, companies will move to more automation—robots. You can read about the next solution in Section VI. As capitalism becomes more efficient, it generally requires less labor to produce all the needed goods and services. Of course, this means less customer purchasing power— *demand*. Thus far, capitalism in the United States has solved some of this problem through innovation and the creation of new goods and services, some of which did not exist a few years ago. But, successful capitalism still might mean a larger government involvement creating quality customers using fiscal and monetary policy. **In the end, *creating quality customers through higher wages is paramount to keeping up demand for goods and services* and completes the recirculation cycle.**

Chapter 16

RECIRCULATION NOT REDISTRIBUTION

Frankly, I think the word "redistribution" is the wrong word to describe this policy. Redistribution should be called "recirculation". The vast majority of government spending, including military, is allocated domestically. Government spending is not hoarded so that its recipients can live on its return. It is spent (recirculated) through the economy. These monies collected by taxes are spread to more individuals, creating more and better consumers. Those who originally get taxed become wealthier, because the recipients of government spending spend it right back into their businesses. There is also the possibility of the government being their customer.

The resistance to the historically proven Keynesian fiscal philosophy of redistribution (recirculation) persists in the current conservative industrial and political leadership (2017). The conservatives resist most types of government spending except military. **By not understanding that it is recirculation and not redistribution, conservatives hinder the creation and improvement of effective recirculation programs. They also reduce the sales revenues of their wealthy constituents (owners).** The conservatives may be politically expedient in supporting certain types of these spending programs, of which Social Security and Medicare are the largest, but by not believing in and, in fact, hindering effective recirculation, they put capitalistic societies in danger from economic depression/recession or outright revolution. The conservatives prevent approving programs, and even more important, they hinder improving on them once they are in operation.

In a free enterprise environment, there is a continual, natural flow of capital to the powerful, the highly educated, and already wealthy by various means—both legal and illegal, or by sheer luck. This natural concentration of wealth continually reduces both the number of businesses and ample individual consumers, eventually hurting commerce and society. All studies, computer models, research, statistics, and macroeconomic history that I have read validate this scenario.

Concentrated wealth, promoted by this flaw of capitalism, creates a system of "The Rich get Richer", for both individuals and businesses. The capitalists/owners dig their own graves by an "infinite accumulation" mentality. This natural bias to the already wealthy reduces competition and the number of adequate consumers. The antitrust laws were established to counter this monopolistic tendency in business enterprises. (See Section III.) The fiscal system of taxing the rich and redistribution (recirculation) back to the many was created to solve this problem on an individual basis.

Adam Smith stated: "Capitalists left to their own devices would rather collude than compete." This means the natural goal of a commercial enterprise is to attain monopoly status, to control or own all or most of their market. (The healthcare industry, medical insurance, and pharmaceutical companies, and commercial banks are prime modern day examples.) This coincides well with the natural goals of many individuals to become as rich as possible. Both Republicans and Democrats have recognized this flaw. In 1890, the Republican Party passed the Sherman Antitrust Act, which was enforced by Republican President, Theodore "Teddy" Roosevelt. (See Section III.) Years later, the Democratic Party started the Keynes fiscal policy of redistribution (recirculation) of income and wealth under Franklin Roosevelt.

Chapter 17

OUTSOURCING IS NOT TRADE

It is fascinating how the much promoted concept of "free trade" has developed considering that the major industrial powers of the 19th, 20th and 21st centuries have been built by using protecting tariffs. Great Britain, the United States, Japan, and now China, all used tariffs to protect their fledgling industries from international competition. China has increased the tactic of administrative burdens, better known as "red tape", to slow the import process besides unfair subsidies and lax environmental regulations. **In fact, with the low tariffs by the U.S., China is basically in a trade war with America. It is not a major news story because we are not fighting!** Congress just complains about the currency manipulation, which is only a symptom of large trade imbalances.

In research over the decades, I have been looking for a short and uncomplicated explanation of trade. I have found one by Paul Craig Roberts in *The Failure of Laissez Faire Capitalism*. I will be paraphrasing his book in this chapter, so I urge all of you to purchase the actual book. Except for monetary reform, he explains our current economic condition in less than 175 pages, and he is from the Reagan administration. Another book to read is *Bad Samaritans: The Myth of Free Trade and the Secret History of Capitalism* by Professor Ha-Joon Chang from Cambridge.

A majority of economists have learned that to question free trade is to be labeled a protectionist. This label could be harmful to their careers. Most have not really researched the theory or its results. The big question: Is outsourcing jobs part of trade, whether free or not?

The theory of free trade was first developed more than 200 years ago by David Ricardo, a bond trader. Unfortunately, he was incorrect then, and even more so now in the modern world where his two necessary conditions of "comparative advantage" are no longer present. In

Ricardo's time, unique national characteristics, climate, and geography were important determinants of relative costs. Today, however, most combinations of inputs that produce outputs are knowledge based. The relative price ratios are the same in every country. Therefore, as opportunity costs do not differ across national boundaries, there is no basis for comparative advantage.

Ricardo's other necessary condition for comparative advantage is that a country's capital seeks its comparative advantage in its home country and does not seek more productive use abroad. Capital has become more mobile than traded goods. Indeed, capital can move with the speed of light, but traded goods have to move by ship or airplane. Approximately half of U.S. imports from China are the offshore production of U.S. firms for the U.S. market.

In the Ricardian free trade model, trade results from countries specializing in different activities where they have a comparative advantage in trading these products for the products of other countries doing likewise. Therefore, trade is not competitive! Countries competing against one another in the same array of products and services are not covered by the Ricardian trade theory.

Offshoring doesn't fit the Ricardian or the competitive idea of free trade. In fact, **offshoring is not trade.** Offshoring is the practice of a firm relocating its production of goods and services from its home market to a foreign country. The main reason is to lower labor costs, and the secondary reason is to lower environmental costs. A third reason to move offshore is to avoid some form of regulation or taxation. Now, it is time to look at what happens economically, using China and the U.S. as examples.

As a function of offshoring, employment and wages have declined in the U.S. Between 1999 and 2011 America lost almost 6 million manufacturing jobs in net terms. This started an increase in unemployment benefits (deficit spending). The unemployed and the underemployed started to search for dollars in order to live or keep the same standard of living. This means that people start borrowing to live or for current spending. These loans are basically credit cards and mortgages. Eventually people cannot support the debt service and the loans stop and/or default. We have the "Great Recession". Then we have to be bailed out by excessive deficit spending and money creation given to the banks by the Federal Reserve.

Wages and employment are increasing in China but **the major issue is the degree of difference!** The basic hourly wage in China was $.71 in 2007 compared to over $20 in the U.S. (It is currently $2.25+ in China, still not enough to be a quality customer.) This was a small step up for the rural poor in China, but they could not buy the products they were making! So, when the U.S. consumer stopped borrowing to buy, there were not enough well paid consumers in China to pick up the slack. As a result, China had to go into excessive deficit spending to support their economy.

The goals of microeconomic thinking and macroeconomic thinking are basically opposed to each other. Therefore, **wage differentiation tariffs are needed more for the protection of our consumers and our industries.** In fact, if we have closer wage parity (it does not have to be equal), limited environmental differences, or excessive government financial support, we could have nominal tariffs between nations. This means that we should probably have low or no tariffs between Japan and Europe and higher tariffs between low slave wage countries and countries whose required environmental costs are significantly lower.

Outsourcing's proponents claim that the lost incomes from job losses are offset by benefits to consumers from lower prices. Allegedly, the harm done to those who lose their jobs is more than offset by the benefit consumers in general get from the alleged lower prices. Yet, proponents are unable to cite studies that support this claim. The claim is based on the unexamined assumption that offshoring is free trade and thereby mutually beneficial. Free traders point out that it lowers prices on TVs, phones, and clothing. But, this neglects the higher costs of education, healthcare, childcare, electricity, gasoline, and so on. Plus, the poor foreign workers are not able to buy a sufficient amount of goods and services to keep their domestic economy moving and substantially increase their standard of living.

Proponents of jobs offshoring also claim that the Americans who are left unemployed soon find equal or better jobs. This claim is based on the assumption that the demand for labor ensures full employment, and that people whose jobs have been moved abroad can be retrained for new jobs that are equal to or better than the jobs that were lost. This claim is false! Offshoring affects all tradable goods and services. The nonfarm payroll data collected by the U.S. Bureau of Labor Statistics makes it clear that in the 21st century, the U.S. economy has been able to create net new jobs only in non-tradable domestic services. Such employment is lowly paid compared to high value-added manufacturing and professional services. (Tradable goods and services are those that can be exported or that are substitutes for imports. Non-tradable goods and services are those that only have domestic markets and no import competition.)

Some offshoring apologists go so far as to imply, and others even claim, that offshore outsourcing is offset by "insourcing". For example, they point out that the Japanese have built car plants in the United States. This is a false analogy. These car plants are an example of direct foreign investment. The Japanese produce in the U.S. in order to sell in the U.S. The plants are a response to Reagan era import quotas on Japanese cars and to high transport costs. They are not producing cars in the United States for the purpose of sending them back to Japan to be marketed. They are not using cheaper American labor to produce for the Japanese home market. At least not yet! They are using cheap Chinese labor.

Many feel that labor should be subject to supply and demand. This is again microeconomic thinking, not macroeconomic thinking, because these laborers are the customers, clients, consumers, and citizens of a country and now the globe. There are hundreds of millions of human laborers who we do not need to produce all the needed goods and services; therefore, they are not quality consumers! Basic wage and fringe benefits should not be subject to supply and demand, because if the demand for labor (and pay) is reduced, so are customers. This becomes self-feeding, continually reducing the demand until the government steps in.

The growing number of displaced and discouraged unemployed Americans is a cost to taxpayers, and family or friends, who provide unemployment insurance, private relief and welfare benefits, and on the viability of the American political and economic system. This cost far exceeds the excessive benefits to a few corporate executives and extra profits to shareholders. In fact, domestic gross revenues (sales) are down!

We should be bringing the global economy up to our standard of living, like we did with Europe and Japan. Instead, these policies are bringing us down to their level! Review Section V, Chapter 22 for more discussion on trade and globalization.

Summary of Solutions

The following are the solutions for increasing the number of customers, clients, and consumers:

1. Install wage differentiation tariffs against low wage countries to encourage significant increases in offshore customers
2. Install **a quality customer minimum wage** for the entire country
3. Encourage labor union development for the private sector with proper regulation and oversight for their operations. Wages and fringe benefits within a competitive industry should be relatively the same!
4. Develop universal employment contracts for all
5. **Provide for more government financing of services to reduce wage pressures on businesses (See Section VI)**
6. **Make sure people have enough money to spend (See Section VI)**
7. Decrease payroll taxes on employees making less than $130,000
8. **Reduce competition on living wages and fringe benefits**
9. Start reducing the 40-hour work week, increasing vacation, sick, and personal leave
10. Increase the ability to retire early

SECTION III

Not Enough Competition

"A completely unregulated market will eventually become a monopoly or at best an oligopoly, thus eliminating the market place."

Chapter 18

INCREASING COMPETITION

There is no such thing as "free markets". That is why I call them "competitive markets". All real markets are political institutions in which some form of market masters, usually government, regulate economic competition among different groups within a society.

On August 31st 1910, Republican Theodore Roosevelt delivered a fiery speech in Kansas. The former president celebrated the extraordinary new commercial power but also gave warning that America's industrial economy had been taken over by a handful of corporate giants that were generating an unparalleled wealth for a small number of people and exercising a growing control over America's politics. Roosevelt cautioned that the country founded on the principle of equal opportunity was in danger of becoming a land of corporate privilege, and pledged to do whatever he could to bring the new giants under control.

In the 1970's the U.S. reduced enforcement of our antitrust laws because they subscribed to the tenets of laissez-faire economics. The laissez-faire libertarians believe that the market place is perfect and self-adjusting. Libertarians have no problem with ever-increasing mergers and acquisitions that create monopolies and oligopolies. Therefore, we have seen a massive consolidation of firms in many industries along with cartels and collusion. Unfortunately, human institutions, operations, and conduct are not perfect or self-adjusting; so, when taken into account, Libertarians contradict their economic theories because a lack of antitrust eliminates or severely reduces the marketplace.

A study by the Economist Magazine in 2016 divided the U.S. economy into 900-odd sectors covered by the five yearly economic censuses and found that two-thirds of them were more concentrated in 2012 than 1997. The weighted average share of the total held by the leading four firms in each sector rose from 26% to 32%.

It is assumed that firms are perfectly competitive; that is, it has been assumed that firms take as a given, the price at which they can sell their output. This is far from the case in the modern economy, where firms have considerable market and political power and can determine their own pricing policies. Few firms are pure monopolists, since they face competition, but they know that how much they can sell depends on the price they set; they are *monopolistically competitive.*

These monopolies and oligopolies reduce competition, which produces many economic negatives. These market conditions cause a reduction in product quality, in employment, in innovation, in investments, in research & development expenditures, and in free exchanges of goods and services by rendering supply chains and complex systems highly fragile. Monopolies increase prices, regulation requirements, reduce new business formations, bankruptcies, and inequality. Monopolies and oligopolies can and do destroy properties and liberties. Excessive consolidations suppress personal income and benefits resulting in less purchasing power of our customers (see Section II). Adam Smith wrote that monopolies raise prices, suppress wages, distort investment, unsettle international relations, pervert the functioning of markets, and are enemies of good management. He also wrote that monopolists, sometimes, destroy men, governments, and nations.

There are many types of monopolies and oligopolies. They are labeled as follows: Horizontal, Vertical, Home Base, Pincer, Railroad, Trading, Privatized Public, Leapfrog, and Futures. I have invented a new one; I call it the Financial Oligopolies. Because of the concentration of monetary power (ability to borrow) along with successful fundraising, a small number of private equity organizations own and control a great number of our businesses. In 2013, these private equity backed companies controlled 23% of America's midsize companies and 11% of its larger companies. Carlyle has 275 companies in their portfolio employing 725,000. KKR's 115 companies employ 715,000. These numbers of employees make them bigger employers than any listed American company other than Walmart.

A complete description of monopolies and their market powers is too lengthy to be enumerated here. You should read *Cornered* by Barry C. Lynn. This is one of the best, current books on the subject. You will see in this book how vast and complicated this topic is, besides its obvious effect on the current, gradual elimination of competitive markets. Also, visit the **American Antitrust Institute's** website.

Unchecked, these unregulated so-called "free markets" are bringing global economies down at an alarming rate. Therefore, the government needs to vastly expand its antitrust division in the Justice Department. We need a large staff to research markets, and to create and enforce adequate regulations to target anticompetitive schemes and predatory contact. They have to make sure they are not too aggressive in their enforcement or too weak. Decisions have to be made about whether a company or group of companies has excessive market power. Antitrust should be returned to its original purpose of achieving market competition, which does reduce the political influence of the money powers. Antitrust regulators have to determine when to break up companies or just regulate. It is a tricky business. Prudent policymakers must reinvent antitrust for the digital age. That means being more alert to the long-term consequences of large firms acquiring promising startups. It means making it easier for consumers to move their data from one company to another, and preventing tech firms from unfairly privileging their own services on platforms they control. And it means making sure that people have a choice of ways of authenticating their identity online. For more input, I suggest that you review the works of Nobel Prize-winning economist, Jean Tirole, at the Toulouse School of Economics in France.

Special attention should be directed to the current financial system's consolidation. The ability to raise and/or create money with a relationship or outright ownership of a commercial bank allows these financiers to become absentee owners. They have so much money at their disposal that they can easily buy up companies and even corner or control markets. Their objectives are usually to maximize short-term profits and/or cash to the detriment of long-term profits, thereby, creating economic destruction. With the implementation of true monetary reform in Section I, there will be more capital available for investment to more people expanding the competitive environment.

This is why it is very important to have an adequate antitrust policy and enforcement. The more competition, the better! **Competition creates more employment, which creates more customers. It rewards efficiency with profits, and inefficiencies with losses. It sharpens management's efforts, improves quality, and increases innovation. It also helps reduce excess inflation. This makes it more difficult for individuals and businesses to gain monopolistic control of the marketplace. Diffusing power and redistributing market share is essential to creating a healthy business environment. If we cannot have this multi-firm free market competition, then we have to regulate the monopolies and oligopolies, including prices, like the public utilities.**

Another related issue is excessive regulations to enter an industry or profession. This cuts competition, creating a smaller market place. Hindering entry by laws and regulations always needs to be reviewed in terms of excluding qualified individuals and business formations from participating in an industry. Online banking will aid in the lowering of these barriers. Modern technology will increase competition by lowering barriers in other industries. In addition, the Antitrust Division has to insure government agencies, both local and federal, do not favor big businesses over small, like the SEC-FINRA. They do this by implementing burdensome and expensive regulations and audits, which are more difficult on the less wealthy, forcing them out of business, thereby reducing competition. Also, larger companies have attained significant market share by putting up barriers through contracts, duration of patents, and copyrights, intellectual property, litigation, and lobbyists. We definitely need easier entry into the commercial banking industry. Online banking will aid in the lowering of these barriers. There is an excellent discussion of this with examples in Chapter 5, 6 & 20 of Robert Reich's new book, *Saving Capitalism*.

Chapter 19

ENHANCING COMPETITIVE MARKETS – CAPITALISM

Enhancing the system of capitalism increases the total tax revenue, which helps the government provide the services that are needed. The government should pursue policies that encourage and facilitate business formations, operations and competition. Local and national governments need to reduce or maintain low barriers to the formation of new businesses—thereby encouraging entrepreneurship.

The government can also play a key role in entrepreneurship by improving the environment for entry and operations. All government policies need to limit hindering incentives, initiative, innovation, productivity, investment, research and development. The government always needs to continually simplify tax laws and regulations—in other words, red tape—in order to facilitate the business marketplace. **Regulators should not over-regulate the good but instead look more for the bad and increase their punishments.** Government needs to insure a level playing field in the business marketplace to insure fair competition.

The government must discourage labor competition within an industry and geographical area based on the cost of basic living expenses, as this will reduce the quality of customers. (See Section VI for the complete solution.) Government regulations need to insure labor utilization, proper incentives and flexibility of hiring and firing while protecting employee rights and unemployment benefits. Regulations need to create portability of benefits, income tax averaging and other features for today's more mobile labor force. Government policy can boost productivity by investing in infrastructure and creating more accessible and affordable quality education for all; thus, creating a more capable labor force.

Businesses need governments! Governments provide the legal systems and the basic security that allow companies to operate in the first place.

They also educate the workers, on whom the firms depend, and they create infrastructure—roads, railways and air traffic control—that enables companies to get their goods to market. Moreover, governments undertake a lot of scientific research that business can turn into commercial products, from the Internet to satellite positioning systems, to drug development. In many industries governments are significant customers.

Freeing up the money system (Section I) can provide additional capital for smaller or new businesses. It is very difficult to compete by matching the purchasing clout and pricing power of global giants along with their ability to handle excessive regulations.

Chapter 20

REGULATING MONOPOLIES AND OLIGOPOLIES

There are certain companies and products that have monopoly status and cannot be broken up. Thus, there has to be some form of regulation that includes pricing and collusion. The perfect example of this is the utility commissions regulating rates, handling customer complaints and various forms of oversight. We need to implement commissions to oversee monopolies and certain oligopolies. These oversight commissions do not have to be at the federal level, most of the current utility commissions are at the local level. Monopolies can also be assessed an excess profit tax to offset lack of competition.

Examples of these monopolies are Monsanto, various drugs and certain healthcare providers such as large hospitals, and health insurance companies in certain geographical areas, Bank of America, Alcoa, credit card companies, and many more.

Besides commissions, there can be certain laws passed and enforced to increase competition. An example is the inability of Medicare to shop pharmaceuticals. We should have a law that states pharmaceutical companies cannot charge greater than 10% more than they charge countries like Japan, UK and Germany. Why should we subsidize these rich countries with our higher prices funding their pharmaceutical's R & D? There is also limited competition that makes sure the company's prices do not decline by involuntary indirect collusion. It is difficult for regulators to prove collusion; a solution would be to actually cap the prices they can charge. Therefore, increased competition and possible regulatory commissions will reduce the amount of collusion.

Summary of Recommendations

1. Change the name of the Antitrust Division in the justice system to the Competitive Division, like in Europe. Always attempt to keep money interests from influencing this department.
2. Drastically increase the number of researchers, economists and attorneys in the Antitrust Division in order to create thoughtful, well-researched, contemporary enforcement. Currently, the Antitrust has been going after technology companies, which are more difficult to judge, and letting our basic industries consolidate, like health insurance, communications, and food.
3. This agency should initiate more monopolization cases in order to target firms that have abused or unfairly acquired their monopoly power.
4. Scrutinize and discourage more mergers and acquisitions.
5. Encourage other countries to use our research and enforcement to increase competition.
6. Develop commissions to regulate monopolies and certain oligopolies.
7. Make it easier for start-ups and smaller firms to access investment capital (See Section I).
8. Reduce regulations – red tape – especially on smaller firms.
9. Review the operational licensing procedures that protect certain industries.
10. Pass legislation that overturns the antitrust law favoring of monopolies.

SECTION IV

Not Enough Long-Range Planning

"The longer you're in business the more profits you will make."

"Fraud and deceptive practices are very profitable in the short run."

Chapter 21

LONG-TERM PROFITS VS. SHORT-TERM PROFITS

There is an obsession with immediate short-term maximization of profits. In short, "The Quick Buck." Private capital (Wall Street) and management are constantly expecting relatively quick and high rates of return. Government capital is more long-term and not profit oriented, so it works more for the benefit of society, including business. We see this clearly in the investments in infrastructure, education, research, and other necessary projects. Government regulations and tax policies should always encourage more long range planning in the private sector. Long range planning is a difficult policy to regulate without overly interfering and restricting operations. But, there are some policies that our leaders, both elected and non-elected, can enact to encourage dual planning in the short-term and the long-term.

An excellent example of encouraging long-term planning in the private sector is tax policy on dividends. Dividends should be taxed at the same rate to individuals as wages are, with a small exclusion for lower income earners. However, dividends should be deductible to the corporations, the same as interest on their debt. This tax change would encourage more equity rather than debt, and dividend payouts instead of accumulation. This new policy will have a tremendous effect on managers, who will now try to maintain the dividend over a longer time period, resulting in better long-range policies than short-term profits for current stock trading. This change can be tax revenue neutral. **Generally, a business will make substantially more money over time because it survives longer with appropriate long-range plans and operations.** One can see the trail of bankrupt businesses over the decades because of the lack of long-range planning. Another advantage for using equity instead of debt is that interest payments are mandatory, while dividend payments are not and can be stopped or reduced.

The way CEOs are currently compensated has a lot to do with reinforcing a companies' short-term profit obsession. CEOs receive stock options in their pay package to incentivize them to increase the value of their stock more in the short run during their tenure. We need to look at ways to change this compensation to use long-range evaluations. Making dividends tax-deductible helps, but maybe some long-term stock that cannot be sold for 10 years will allow the executive and his family to benefit from dividends and future appreciation. Stocks with long-term holding requirements can have more voting rights as France's Florange Law.

Current management initiates stock repurchase programs which reduces the amount of stock thus increasing the earnings per share without adding any value to the corporation. This policy is initiated so their stock and stock options have greater value when they sell. Therefore the amount of stock purchased should be controlled and restricted either by law, board of directors, or securities regulations.

A change of accounting systems, such as life cycle accounting, can also encourage long-term planning. It can increase planning from three to five years to 30 to 100 years, as is done in Japanese companies.

Businesses need to do dual planning. Management must keep their eye on the short-term picture, making sure to achieve their growth and profit objectives. Management must also implement their long-term investment plan for profitable growth and sustainability. They should not be interested in trading short-term profit for long-term growth and profitability. Companies need to be focused on building long-term enduring relationships with their customers, employees, shareholders, and the wider community. Management owners should not be fooled by short-term profit maximization. Companies that pay their employees well can also have high-profits. The lack of long-range planning is why there is only one company left on the original Dow Jones 30 and less than 15% on the original Standards & Poor 500 from their inception in 1923!

Pollution is another notable example. Does it pay to maximize short-term profits by disregarding appropriate pollution controls, resulting in costly cleanups, fines, and possible extinction; not to mention killing your customers or making them sick so they have to spend more on healthcare instead of your company's goods and services? No, it does not. Pollution controls greatly enhance the long-term benefits not only to people, but to all businesses.

A great example of short-term planning was the current financial crisis. The banks/mortgage companies and Congress wanted more people housed, so the private banking system came up with subprime loans which substantially raised the borrower's payment after two years. This large increase in such a short period of time did not allow the borrower the ability to make the payments which resulted in foreclosures. These foreclosures caused losses for the homeowners, banks, investors, and the world. What lenders should have done to make more money in the long term is issue participating, fixed rate, home mortgages where lenders could have received 10%, 20% or 30 % of the profits upon sale, refinance or gifting. This would have yielded more revenue to the lenders than the subprime commissions, rather than going bankrupt and having to be bailed out by the government and the Federal Reserve.

Remember, the total of long-term profits, by staying in business longer, should always be greater than the sum of all short-term profits added together! Long-term planning, yielding long-term profits for both business and the community is the most sustainable economic model over time.

Summary of Recommendations

1. Make dividends tax deductible to the C Corporation (See Corp. Tax in Section V.)
2. Alter CEO and other executives' pay to encourage more long-range planning.
3. Control and restrict stock repurchase programs
4. All community leaders, both elected and nonelected, should use the bully pulpit to encourage more long range planning
5. Encourage more Corporate Social Responsibility Programs (See Section V.)

SECTION V

Other Economic Topics

"Adding My Two Cents."

Chapter 22

GLOBALIZATION AND TRADE

Globalization is the continual increase and expansion of commerce by individual firms worldwide. As a consequence, globalization produces the gradual elimination of national boundaries, where commerce is concerned. However, these global firms are basically in competition with each other, not with individual countries. Although there are certain larger firms that are government owned and or supported, especially in China. Cross border commerce has generated both positive and negative effects. The major flaws of capitalism have followed globalization and must be dealt with on an international level.

There are limited international regulatory bodies to oversee these firms with the exception of the World Trade Organization, which does not have much power and favors big business over countries and customers. Obviously, we will need to develop more institutions for this purpose. It will be a major task for future administrations to comprehensively address these issues. So, how can we compete as a nation when our firms and other countries' firms buy, sell and produce all over the world to take advantage of these flaws in capitalism? We cannot! Therefore, the major area of concern for our government is and should be the economic well-being of our people, our customers. This concept of a well compensated work force, creating quality consumers, is a major objective of every nation. **In order to rebalance global trade and wages, we must have the wages of the international workforce progress *towards us* and *not* ours being lowered to theirs.**

Countries like China are attempting to compete as a country not as independent businesses. The government owns many of their larger companies. This is a socialist scheme, *not capitalism*. China competes by making use of flaw number two, outlined in Section II. China is taking advantage of the huge consumer base (middle class) in the United States and Europe. The major long run problem with this strategy is that it is not building a large enough adequate consumer base in China. This is why the Chinese government has significant domestic spending and excessive inventories. If U.S. consumers slightly lower their consumption due to lower wages, less credit card usage, less home equity line debt usage or if there was a basic recession, China could see a significant recession/depression.

Since the U.S. is still a primary customer, it has the power to use tariff changes, not to protect industries, but to protect the population's purchasing power. More importantly, to force low wage countries to pay an adequate wage so they can become adequate consumers. We do not have to insist on equal wages, but *reasonable non slave* labor wages that will continue to rise in order to allow access into our markets. Yes, minimum wages and Labor Unions are an additional method to help accomplish an adequate consumer base goal, but a wage differential tariff changes are needed as well.

A paper by Justin Pierce, of the Federal Reserve, and Peter Schott of Yale, argues that joining the WTO (World Trade Organization) removed the risk for China of steep increase in U.S. tariffs, making it less perilous for its companies to invest in new factories. The authors found that industries where the treat of tariff increases was most reduced suffered the greatest job losses in the U.S.

The concept of Americans having super cheap goods and services, which offsets our wage declines, is absurd. This differential, so we can buy 10 shirts instead of nine, is not economically justified when those workers, who make the shirts, can't buy any of our production of goods and services. Furthermore, the increase in the labor component of manufacturing in other countries will not significantly raise prices to alter our consumer habits. We should eliminate or reduce all tariffs on countries that have adequate wages and environmental practices. We should raise tariffs on all those who do not. We should also consider a tiny (1-2%) general tariff on all goods as a revenue raising structure, in addition to taxes.

The excessive trade deficit is deceiving to some degree as well. The trade deficit does not include monies coming into the United States in terms of education of foreign students, investments in stocks, real estate and government bonds. Other countries receive our paper and we receive their goods and services. What it does mean is that foreign individuals, enterprises and countries will own our assets as we will own theirs. This is true globalization! How do we compete in this environment? The solution is to reduce our dependence on foreign oil, which we have, and create an increase in the wages of other countries, through wage tariff increases, so their workers can afford to buy our goods and services.

The "Fair Trade vs. Free Trade" argument is somewhat bogus, because almost all industrialized countries have some sort of tariffs. I am for free trade with the proper tariffs to protect the consumer base wage differentials, ecological differences, and anticompetitive practices (dumping & subsidies) by governments with large pocket books. Our firms can compete with any firm globally; they only need a relatively level playing field. You can review the Trade Section in Section II, it belongs here too.

Implementing true monetary reform (Section I), will eliminate or substantially reduce the need for government borrowing bonds. The countries with positive trade balances (exports exceed imports) will generally have the stronger currencies with a limited ability to manipulate their currencies. It will also hinder trade by many of the less productive countries to purchase the goods and services of the countries in positive balance. This is similar to the way it is today.

To overcome this trade problem, an international mechanism has to be established to gift back currencies to the trade deficit countries. This will allow those deficit countries to continue to trade with the positive trade balances countries. These deficit countries just spend it right back in to the positive countries' economies! This gifting stimulates trade and stabilizes both countries' currency! Remember, it is only money that costs nothing to produce except excess inflation which has already been reduced by the positive trade balances. There will have to be percentages developed to implement the transfers. Essentially it is similar to foreign aid.

The world's exchange rates will totally change as the Mandell-Fleming trilemma will be eliminated. This is known as the impossible or inconsistent trinity that says a country must choose between free capital mobility, exchange rate management and monetary autonomy. The U.S. currency is the current major reserve currency that will be used less as a reserve but is still the major trading currency for a lot of other reasons. (See "Biography of the Dollar" by Craig Karmin.)

If a country's currency gets so strong (Dutch disease) that it hinders exporting companies to compete around the globe, there can be another mechanism to give them a small percentage of cash so they can lower prices to be competitive in the global marketplace. This is not the huge subsidies that allow them to undercut the competition which is used by certain countries to become market dominant.

Chapter 23

TAXES

There are many websites, newsletters, books, etc. on tax policy. Following are only the general important concepts and the defense of progressive tax policy.

The Progressive Income Tax is one of the fairest taxes, as it is based solely on the ability to pay. What is important is not how much any individual earns, but how much is left over to be an adequate consumer and save for retirement. This bears repeating: It is not important how much one pays in taxes, but how much money is left *after paying taxes*! Creating quality consumers is essential to tax policy and, therefore, the Progressive Income Tax is the key to sound government fiscal policy creating the proper amount of recirculation, offsetting flaw number two: not enough customers (Section II).

If substantially more current fiscal programs are funded through a diversified monetary system (See Section I), we can actually lower the income and payroll tax brackets and still balance the fiscal budget without hurting the economy! This creates even better customers, clients, and consumers. It allows wage earners to buy more homes, save for retirement, and buy more goods and services, which will cause an economic boom. This increased economic activity will increase total business tax revenues. Tax deductions and credits can also be used to offset business risk and encourage social behavior.

INCOME TAXES & PAYROLL TAXES

Of course, actually, rates and tax policy is the prerogative of Congress. The following will give you and Congress an idea of what the tax brackets should be with proper monetary reform. These brackets are based on taxable income (after all deductions) and it **includes an individual's payroll taxes, and taxes on dividends.** They are also not retroactive. **(Dividends need to be taxed the same as any other income. Capital gains are different.**)

- $0 – $50,000 NO **income or payroll taxes – This income figure probably can go higher!**
- $50-100,000 5% (With monetary reform, this figure should go to zero, too.)
- $100-150,000 10%
- $150-200,000 15%
- $200-250,000 20%
- $250-300,000 25%
- $300-350,000 30%
- $350-400,000 35%
- $400-500,000 40%
- $500-999,000 45%
- Over $1,000,000 50%

This would give a tax bracket cut to over 99% of the U.S. population! It also assumes some form of monetary reform has been implemented.

Should the tax on dividends be so substantially below the taxes on interest and wages? The answer is – no. Dividends should be taxed to the individual at the same rate as everything else with exclusion for a small amount of dividends and interest, in order to stimulate and help lower income families save for retirement. In fact, the dividends paid out by corporations should be tax deductible with offsetting increases in taxes to make it revenue neutral. This will encourage corporations to plan more for the long term, which addresses flaw number four in Section IV. These increased dividend payments will help the Baby Boomer Bubble through retirement without any requirement to sell their stocks.

Payroll-FICA-Social Security Tax is actually an income tax. It needs to be included in any income tax debate as more workers pay a higher payroll tax than income tax. It is not as progressive as the income tax because it is a flat tax with a ceiling. A great tax cut for 95% of the workers and many small businesses in the country would be a reduction in the employee based tax rate and elimination of the ceiling. This could be structured to be revenue neutral or a revenue increase to actually extend social security.

Decreasing the number of brackets and itemized deductions is NOT tax simplification! The computer handles all those simple calculations. Also, many do not even itemize, and of those who do, most do not reach the threshold to even deduct medical, casualty, and miscellaneous deductions. The key to simplification is the above the line calculations that have to be done before it reaches the computer; such as eliminating the AMT calculations, simplify real estate write off rules, separation of capital gains taxes, have K-1s become 1099s.

CAPITAL GAINS TAXES

Collectability in tax legislation always has to be considered in specific tax regulations and laws. The capital gains rate at 20% is substantially below the maximum wage rate at 39%. But, the lower the capital gains rate, usually, more transactions and less deferral strategies, result in more total tax revenues. But, some use this argument to keep lowering the rate. If it becomes 0%, there will be zero collections!

The capital gains tax rate should be progressive with 5-15% for the smaller amounts and 20-35% for the very large amounts. This would drastically increase revenue, as everyone in the stock market would be selling (and buying back) smaller amounts at the end of the year for a tax gain at the lower rates. The very large transactions usually do not have a strategy of waiting, but all the deferral and elimination loopholes need to be reviewed. One that should be eliminated is the "stepped up in cost basis" on the spouse's death. The actual capital gains tax calculation should **not** be integrated with the other taxes, as it is now, but have a separate page within the return.

ESTATE TAXES

The estate tax is also a very fair tax because the taxpayer is dead and no longer in need of their money. It is levied only on the very, very rich. Estate tax is the best tax to offset the second flaw in Section II—the rich getting richer—which reduces the number of consumers and the ability to build wealth. Importantly, there are provisions to help family farms and businesses and a healthy gifting allowance. Contrary to some opinions, many of these assets have never been taxed! The estate tax reduces "Economic Royalty" which eventually causes the economy and society to fail. **It would be a macroeconomic disaster to eliminate the estate tax.** Even today with estate taxes, we see an extreme over concentration of wealth in just a few families. **Recirculation, of some of the assets, is absolutely necessary for a successful capitalistic system.** (See Section II.)

The current Reagan Era Estate Tax structure is actually very reasonable. The structure eliminates all taxes on most estates. The current structure just needs to be more progressive with lower starting rates and higher rates for the extremely wealthy, which is only about .01%-.03% of the U.S. population. We should always debate the proper estate tax rates and exclusions. The current position of the right is *elimination*, which is totally wrong; and the lower exclusions by the left are too low. The left does not realize that we need investment from private capital; the government can't do it all. History is full of examples of rich men with big ideas; i.e. Elon Musk, Sergey Brin, Howard Hughes, Richard Branson, and Peter Thiel.

CORPORATE TAXES

Collectability in corporate taxation is a major issue. The U.S. currently has a 35% corporate tax rate, which many of the major and global corporations substantially reduce by offshore maneuvers and corporate tax deductions. These corporations will always hire the most competent lawyers and CPAs to give them tax reduction advantage. These tax reduction tactics are actually a disadvantage for smaller corporations that use the C Corporation structure, because they can't afford to make use of these tax reduction strategies. The solution for these smaller corporations is to have the tax brackets become more progressive.

The U.S. has one of the highest tax rates in the world. Instead of fighting offshore tax havens, we should join them! The U.S. should have a 10-15% net profit rate for all C Corporations Tax shelter maneuvers become too expensive to implement with this low rate and the U.S. becomes a corporate tax haven. You will see foreign companies move to the U.S. to receive the many other benefits of this country. We would replace the lost revenue by eliminating some of the extravagant loopholes and by adding an approximate 1 - 5% tax on **gross profits from domestic revenues** on **all** corporations and businesses (foreign & domestic). Gross profits are easier to calculate than net profits. Tax revenues will increase, because the U.S will be taxing foreign based companies and there will be no tax on foreign sales (exports).

If we don't change to this system, then corporate tax rates should be more progressive because corporations have a greater ability to pay, as their taxes are based on profits after salaries and expenses. The tax rate should be lowered for smaller and less profitable businesses and increased on more profitable corporations. Of course, the very significant corporate loophole system and offshore havens always need to be reviewed and corrected, which will allow actual rates to become lower without losing revenue.

Lowering or raising income taxes does not necessarily create a boom or bust. There are many other factors involved. Most of these taxes are usually spent into the economy by the government. The Clinton Administration raised taxes in the early 1990s and we had the biggest boom in the history of mankind. The income tax rate in the early 1930s, during the Hoover Administration, was 24% only paid by the few very wealthy, and we had the worst depression in modern industrial history. Of course, some government taxing system can be too confiscatory resulting in overly restricting and reducing the incentives of the free enterprise system. The U.S. individual income tax rates, excluding payroll taxes, are one of the lowest in the industrialized world.

In other words, a tax rate of 99% is too high and 1% is far too low to overcome the flaws of capitalism. The Clinton years seem to depict an appropriate level of taxation. Personal and corporate tax rules, regulations and preparation should be kept as simple as possible. This does not mean reducing the number of brackets or itemized deductions, but mostly the above the line regulations.

One has to be careful with taxes based on sales not profits such as sales taxes, consumption taxes, the Value Added Tax and property taxes. They can over interfere with commerce and are usually over burdensome for lower income families and businesses.

The financial transaction tax or Tobin tax (FFT) is a very tiny per dollar charge on every financial transaction. This tax is an excellent tax because it is very small and hits mainly the wealthy; while reducing the cheating of high frequency trading. It also creates a check on excesses that produce a financial bubble. The problem with the Tobin tax is that it would only work if it was implemented around the globe especially in New York and London as traders would move to financial centers without the tax. A recent paper by Marcos Chamon, of the IMF and Mario Garia, of the PUC-RIO, suggests that the Tobin Tax would be effective in controlling extreme inflows and outflows of capital between countries. This would increase the financial stability reducing the risk of currency collapses.

There is an argument that individuals end up paying all taxes either directly or through high prices. Although this statement is somewhat true because we are all in the economic system, it is an unrelated argument, because pricing mechanisms include many costs and other factors of which taxes are only one. Taxation comes out at various points of the production (wages), sales (sales tax), and profit (income tax) cycle. The question is: at what point does it come out? Remember, with a well diversified, non debt based monetary system, tax revenues can be lowered. Also, tax increases at the Federal level decrease the money supply in circulation, and Federal spending increases the supply.

Chapter 24

EDUCATION

Education is very important to individuals in a capitalistic system—especially math and science in our high tech world. Education is also very important to a democratic society in general. But, education is only one of the important components for a successful economy. Brazil, Russia, and India, before recent economic booms, had well educated populations with nominal success economically.

What is important in the United States is that we must begin to educate the general population in matters of personal finance and capitalism. We live in a capitalistic society and world. The more educated the public is, the less reliant they will be on government programs. **Every high school student should be required to take a course in personal financial planning in order to graduate.** The College of Financial Planning and others have excellent personal high school level financial planning courses, and many CFPs would volunteer to teach them. Getting a financial planning education can help to reduce inequality.

Individuals need to rely on themselves not just the government to reduce their inequality. Individuals need to consider pooling their talents and funds with friends and family in starting businesses, investment funds, and owning real estate properties. Consider the same pooling for volume buying of goods and services. The less income you have the more consumer aware you need to be to lower your expenses to create savings. I know it is difficult working together in these areas but there are legal and managerial materials to help in joint efforts. These recommendations are private solutions for reducing inequality by not relying totally on the government.

Since money can be created at no cost by the government, except for excess inflation, and education is a primary social and business policy, the government can make long-term college loans – 20 to 30 years – at a cost of about 1-2%, with repayment starting after graduation. The interest charge just covers administration costs and defaults. The government does not have to make a profit and it does not matter how long it takes to be repaid, as long as it is repaid. This allows almost everyone to afford a student loan and relieves the burden on the fiscal side of government. **The problem is that the college system keeps raising costs higher than the inflation rate because of the access to these loans.** This results in overburdening students to the detriment of the economy. We have to control these costs with a regulated tuition. I recommend that 99% of all public schooling be mostly free to all from preschool through university. We can always require some public service for the advanced education.

Chapter 25

STATISTICS & FORMULAS

Have you ever noticed that the economic academics and pundits on television and in print are very confusing, opaque, and paradoxical? They use terms to describe the status of an economy that are nebulous and have defused meanings; words like growth, growth rate, and GDP (Econo-speak). Economists also never use the word "people" or their condition in describing an economy.

Beware of economic statistics and formulas. They reduce human economic conditions to numbers and we rely too heavily on their accuracy for macroeconomic decision-making. Macroeconomic formulas and statistics can be unreliable from errors in collection, and they can be interpreted in many different ways. Most of the economists do not agree on their own definitions of such things as growth and productivity. The savings statistics are also misleading. Savings statistics do not include pension contributions and subtract them when they are paid out. They also do not include investments. The highest savings rate in the world is in Japan, which has been in a recession for 25 years, according to GDP. **The inflation statistics are the most important**. Since the cost of producing money is basically the inflation rate, we have to carefully monitor these statistics to insure a reasonable amount of monetary creation.

Let's discuss this Growth Domestic Product (GDP), which is always cited when discussing the condition of an economy. The following is the basic definition:

"The total market value of all final goods and services produced in a country in a given year, equal to total consumer, investment and government spending, plus the value of exports, minus the value of imports."

The GDP is increasingly a poor measure of prosperity. The high growth rate nations such as India and China have very high growth rates over the last decade or so. Yet, they still have over 1.5 billion people that are extremely poor. Their environmental conditions are bordering on deadly, and their other services, like medical care, leave something to be desired. (They are improving!) Consider Europe and Japan; they have almost nonexistent growth rates, few dirt-poor people, low cost education, free medical care for all, and a reasonable environment to live in. Where would you prefer to live?

GDP is just a broad measurement of the overall activity of the economy, simply depicting if an economy is up or down. Endless economic statistical growth is not only mathematically ridiculous but leads the world towards disaster. (See "Economics Unmasked" by Smith & Max-Reef.) However, if you look at GDP per head, it might look alright, but it is just *an average*. The millionaires/billionaires bring up the average, so it does not appear if there are any poor; nor does it describe the living conditions of most of the people. The GDP is less reliable when a growing share of the economy consists of services. The GDP does not account for depletion of capital (wear and tear on infrastructure), government assets (roads and parks), and intangible capital (online networks scientific ideas, and skills). It also misses any type of measurement of the quality of the environment. The academic world has attempted to create different measurements formulas describing the well-being of the economy and its people. None of these formulas has ever caught on, so we are still using this archaic term that almost means nothing.

Our main concern is what is economically happening to ALL of the population. **As a businessman, this is in my own self-interest. I want to have everyone be a quality customer or client. I am not even going to discuss how this system will create a quality community for my children and grandchildren to live in.**

You can go to the website http://www.shadowstats.com and determine for yourself the various interpretations of macroeconomic formulas.

Productivity

I need to say a few words about productivity. First, it is mainly a microeconomic term, not a macroeconomic one. Second, economist academia cannot agree on the various formulas. Third, productivity is difficult to measure. Fourth, it relates to labor as a cost not a customer. Fifth, productivity varies among industrial sectors. Sixth, it is necessary to be productive so we can mass produce goods and services, creating the abundance we need at reasonable prices.

However, it has almost nothing to do with consumers being able to afford these goods and services. In fact, unless there was a rare labor shortage, it was not until a quality wage was forced to be paid (forced by minimum wages and unions) that the purchasing power of workers was large enough to purchase these mass produced items. This increased purchasing power gave consumers the ability to start using up the excess capacity of the private sector.

You might have noticed in the "Great Recession" the productivity of our firms vastly improved as employment, financial markets, and consumer spending collapsed!

Chapter 26

OWNERSHIP & CORPORATE SOCIAL RESPONSIBILITY PROGRAMS

Ownership

Ownership should be encouraged for everyone in a capitalistic system. It is very difficult to continue to raise wages so that workers can save and build wealth for retirement (spending). Therefore, the government, to promote ownership by every citizen, should implement laws and regulations that enhance that outcome. Ownership does not have to be actual direct ownership of businesses and real estate properties, but through indirect ownership of stocks, real estate investment trusts, or other investment vehicles. The government should continue to encourage all pensions, profit sharing, Employee Stock Ownership Plans, 401K, and IRA plans. In the long run, it will mean less reliance on government fiscal services. I prefer the government not own any marketplace companies. They can regulate them, but governments have enough to do without making managerial decisions causing unfair and reduced competition.

Corporate Social Responsibility

Many businesses have implemented Corporate Social Responsibility (CSR) programs and strategic planning. These programs are similar to the efforts of charities. CSRs are great programs, but they don't have nearly enough committed capital to make a significant dent in solving the social problems compared to the larger amount that governments can spend on social programs.

 CSRs are really a part of the businesses' marketing programs. There are several reasons for these programs. First, consumers may take this as a signal that the company's products are of high quality. Second, customers may be willing to buy the company's product as an indirect way of donating to their favorite causes. The third reason is the "halo effect" that companies receive when its good deeds earn it greater consideration from consumers and others. The fourth reason is that it makes it easier to attain funds from the international capital markets. Fifth, increase the number of investors in the company and last, it can boost morale of employees.

Studies have shown that there have been more lenient penalties on prosecutions for companies with these programs. Studies have also shown that some of these companies have also avoided taxes. Can you be socially responsible and not pay your taxes?

Chapter 27

USURY

In the not too distant past, certain principles of money were not subject to alteration by society's money managers. They might be ignored or forgotten for a time, but they could not be repealed. One of these principles was the ancient biblical injunction against *usury*. The definition of usury may have vacillated over the centuries, but the moral meaning was the same. *When lenders insisted on terms that were sure to ruin the borrowers, this was wrong.* It was usury. Besides being macro economically unsustainable, it is against every religion in the world!

There were practical, as well as moral reasons why usury was considered a *sin*. Usury was more than a social plea for fairness and generosity from the wealthy. No social system could tolerate usury, not as a permanent condition, because it led to an economic life that was self-devouring. The money monger collected his due until he owned all the property and all the other people had nothing. No one could really survive. Who would buy from the money monger if he had all the money? What kind of life would the general population have?

We have had usury laws in our country. Currently there are none.

Consequently, moneylenders can charge as high a rate of interest as they want; 20%, 30% or more. They say they need these highs rates because of defaults, but **the high rates cause the defaults**! Usury laws capping the highest rate that can be charged using the rates derived from inflationary statistics must be enacted to preserve the buying power of the quality customer and reduce bankruptcies. Those rates must be reasonable for both the lender and the borrower.

Personal borrowing, not investing, should be limited to emergencies and large items like housing, cars, furniture and college. It should not be used to maintain a standard of living, because these people have no means to pay it back.

The question is whether the financial monetary system will promote economic growth and rising living standards, or create unproductive financial credit which uses the government to enforce creditor claims by imposing austerity, reducing a large swath of the world population to debt peonage. The solution is to keep a cap on interest rates of loans or at least certain loans. This cap can be set by the treasury in relationship to the inflation rate.

Chapter 28

ENVIRONMENT

Environmental practices are not contrary to capitalism. In many ways, they lower costs and increase profits especially in the long run. What is contrary to capitalism is the wasting and using up of nonrenewable commodities like oil. It does not make sense to burn this natural resource because it is a valuable non fuel commodity.

There is substantial research with many books on this subject that are easy to locate. Many discuss the inclusion of a pricing system to pay for environmental investments and clean ups. Section I provides low cost funding for both private companies, individuals and governments to implement environmental friendly equipment conversions, repairs, clean ups, conservation measures and other projects. We also need an **environmental differentiation tariff** against those countries that compete by lowering their environmental standards. In the absence of regulation, we over exploit our environment and natural resources.

Our customers, clients, consumers, and citizens cannot live in a polluted environment with an end result that transfers our business sales and profits into the health care or mortuary sector! **The key is to implement the 5Rs: Reuse, Recycle, Repair, Regeneration and Renewables.**

Chapter 29

HEALTHCARE

Obamacare is a lengthy law to mainly regulate the private medical insurance marketplace. This marketplace is dominated by a few large for-profit medical insurance companies whose objective, inadvertently or not, is to lower claims and increase premiums to increase profits. This was not the marketplace back in the 1970's. We had many insurance companies for profit and nonprofits competing for the premium dollars. If a client didn't like the cost or service, they would change companies! This does not exist today. All we needed back in the 70's were basic insurance coverage guarantees and guaranteed issue, dictated by the government, which Obamacare basically does now.

Medical insurance can be a product sold in a competitive marketplace. This is where Section III can help by insuring competition among health insurance companies. Delivering actual medical care is far more difficult to implement in a competitive market place. It is difficult to shop doctors, surgeons, and hospitals, etc.

You can find a lot of research and many books written on this topic with quality solutions. I will give you some ideas that should be considered.

1. Pass the Medicare Productivity Act. There are many quality consultants and academics who have helpful concepts and specifics that Congress can utilize to make healthcare delivery services far **more effective and less expensive**. This includes shopping pharmaceuticals for Medicare Part D. Congress can create a law that does not allow the pharmaceutical companies to charge the U.S. patients more than Europe and Japan. The U.S. needs to stop subsidizing rich nations. **This Act will help Medicare and provide guidelines for the private sector**

2. Significantly increase the assets necessary to search out and prosecute Medicare fraud. This is self-funding by reducing the number of fraudsters

3. Medicare is extremely popular to a large majority of the over 65 population. Insurance companies do not want to insure older people. Because of the oligopoly state of the current private insurance marketplace, the solution is probably Medicare for all. The administration of which could be handled by the private insurance companies, similar to Switzerland, Medicare supplements and Part D. The private insurance companies would market the supplement policies similar to the Medicare Part B supplements with a broader selection. The insurance industry could also have private insurance to sell, for those who do not want Medicare for all

4. We currently have a National Health Service, which is operated like the Military Medical Corps. It should be expanded to cover emergencies and rural areas. In fact, it can be integrated within the domestic military medical operations. Medical personnel can have their education paid for based on years of service to this corps

Chapter 30

REGULATIONS

Regulations are established to protect our customers and clients, as well as businesses. Regulations attempt to create a level playing field in the marketplace and increase transparency. Besides increasing competition (Section III), there are many ways we can continue to improve our regulatory systems. Like all human operations, our regulatory system cannot be perfect. Therefore, the system always needs to be reviewed. **Under our current systems, we tend to over-regulate the good instead of looking for the bad.**

Obviously, this is not a book on regulations, but the following is a laundry list for improvements and even reductions:

1. Important rules should be subjected for a review by an independent watchdog
2. Most major regulations should have a sunset clause to ensure review every ten years
3. Rules need to be much simpler—cleaner
4. Have a rapid appeals process
5. Regulators need to be accountable and can be fired
6. Consider functional regulation; consolidate in smaller agencies and less overlapping regulators
7. Consider principle-based regulations, which lay out a broad set of principles for businesses to follow, instead of laying out what is forbidden and what is allowed
8. Review for macro prudential regulation versus micro based regulation
9. Regulator systems need to be cost efficient and comprehensive

Naming and shaming has become a popular tool for regulators. Policy makers have attempted to influence business practices by exploiting companies' obsession with protecting their brands. The threat of public embarrassment has so far proved more potent than fears of fines. It allows politicians to affect corporate behavior without appearing too heavy handed. It reduces the need to carry out costly regulations and enforcement.

Crime, Corruption & Crony Capitalism

The human systems of commerce work much better with lower levels of criminal activity, bribes taken by government employees, and assets and capital given to well-connected private interests. Of course, it is impossible to eliminate them, but law enforcement, regulators, and our political leaders need to keep them as limited as possible. This includes fairness in contract construction and enforcement, along with upholding private property rights.

A difficult task is to get governments to not participate in illegal acts against companies located in other countries. We all need to abide by the same basic rules for global commerce. Tariffs are a non-military enforcement strategy.

My final recommendation is to increase the funding that goes to searching for and prosecuting fraud and theft. This is basically a Justice Department expansion not a regulatory expansion.

Chapter 31

BUSINESS STRUCTURES AND GOVERNANCE

Some economists think we can improve our economy by changing our business structures to cooperatives and nonprofits. First, this is a microeconomic solution for a macroeconomic problem and almost impossible to implement. I prefer a large selection of different options to increase competition (Section III); these options include nonprofits, associations, cooperatives, C & S Corporations, LLCs, Partnerships and Sole Proprietors, along with employee ownership.

An important factor is to have appropriate governance of these operations. You have seen many public and nonprofit companies where the management controls the business *instead of the owners.* Therefore, there are no checks and balances, resulting in extraordinary salaries and many inappropriate decisions. We need to have effective democratic elections to the Boards of Directors and strengthen the standards around directorships that are important for appropriate oversight. Besides splitting the Chief Executive and Chairman roles can be good for returns and governance.

Chapter 32

SOCIAL SECURITY

A large majority of older Americans depend on Social Security income (SSI) as their majority income source! This allows them to be better quality customers/clients/consumers/citizens.

Currently Social Security is considered a pension and benefit program that is causing difficulties in creating a solution and public understanding. Social Security is NOT an actuarial pension system! It is a recirculation tax and transfer system. SSI takes from the workers making about $118,500 or less (this figure goes up every year) and their employers match this amount. This payroll tax is a regressive tax, not a progressive one.

Therefore, this payroll revenue should not be in a separate box. The revenue should be within the overall budget and collected within a progressive income tax. The tax is too harsh a tax on lower income families. On the income side, the calculation should NOT be totally based on how much one pays in, but how much one needs the income. This is accomplished by having a 100% taxation of the income at the higher income levels and a more standard payout for everyone.

There have been many studies and analysis on how to solve the Social Security income shortage. I have read and reviewed many of them. The following is a list of the most important factors:

1. Increase the payroll tax rate
2. Increase the payroll tax base
3. Tax income like private pensions are taxed
4. Require coverage of state and local employees
5. Allow the trust fund to invest in the private investment market like private pensions
6. Increase the retirement age
7. Impose a gradual Means test on the income

8. Alter CPI cost of living adjustments
9. Reduce benefits across the board for future retirees
10. Increase the number of years used in the income benefit computation

Unfortunately, these solutions only consider the solvency factors. Section I solves this factor by creating money. The solutions do not consider the human and macroeconomic customer factors. We need to explore how to improve Social Security for the workers of America and the overall economy. It is obvious that "one age fits all" does not work for many occupations and excludes most health factors.

One point is the actual statistic of when the system will be bankrupt. The experts keep extending then lowering the date. As of this entry, the date is now 2037. Have you ever noticed that most economic projections over extended periods of time can be very inaccurate? A thirty year projection of insolvency lends itself to being very inappropriate. Attempting to solve something where we do not know the employment, life span and retirement habits, the economic conditions and tax revenues three or four decades from now is probably impossible.

The solution is to merge the Social Security into the entire federal budget fiscal system. The government currently spends all the revenues anyway! Any short falls can be covered by monetary creation.

Let's discuss how to improve Social Security based on human needs which also aids in a more macroeconomic expansion by providing more funds to more people creating better quality customers.

Social Security should benefit the lower income workers, the more occupationally hazardous workers, and the medically impaired workers more than others!

The Social Security age should be lowered to age 60. Workers who have difficult jobs or in poor health (not just the severely disabled) can start earlier. This system can be based on a non-rigged liberal basis so workers can start collecting early based on occupational verification and medical history review. Yes, there will be some who will take advantage but most will need it. Those of us who sit in an office and are healthy and still working will not be able to collect at all until at least age 70 as it was until the 1990's.

Social Security income can still be reduced for earlier retirement and the less one pays into the system, but it would be much better macro economically if the payouts are closer to parity. A poorer worker needs the money substantially more than a wealthy worker. This solution would help more workers than our current system and with more deserving workers having more for consumption activities; it would substantially increase the stimulation of the economy.

Instead of having a means test, it would be more advisable and easier to implement an adjustment to the taxation of the social security income. It should be 100% taxable for higher income brackets. It is currently at 85%. Thus, the less needy pays more back indirectly. This also helps the so-called insolvency problem.

Obviously my suggestions are general in nature. Appropriate economists can research the specific rules, numbers and ages at the time of the proposed legislation. But everyone wins. The poor and medically unfit receive more and the overall economy is improved, by more people having more money.

SECTION VI

The Future

&

Summary of Solutions

"It is Consumerism Not Socialism."

Chapter 33

JOBS ARE DYING

Almost two hundred years ago, the Luddites, were an organized group that violently protested against losing their jobs to the machines during the start of the industrial revolution. The productivity increases did create more jobs but not enough well paying ones to support the dramatic increase in capacity. Therefore, we saw severe recessions and depressions for the next hundred years. They called them "panics" in those years. Yes, we were still far better off than the rest of the world, but most of the population, living then, we would consider today as dirt poor.

These conditions existed all the way to World War II. The main reason was the economists of yesteryear did not equate employees and labor with customers, clients, and consumers. Unfortunately, many economists, business executives, and owners still don't do so today!!

The implemented solutions that changed everything to a better economy and life for a large majority of the population were minimum wage regulations, labor union successes and government jobs and subsidies. In fact, the government subsidies through the GI Bill after the war created the biggest boom in the history of mankind! These policies created a large consumer base, which allowed businesses to use up their capacity and expand from there.

The U.S. and other countries were headed in the right direction by solving the flaws of capitalism until the 1980's. The conservative, reactionary economists decided to move back to the failed policies of the laissez faire economics of the 19th century, instead of correcting the operating mistakes of the 20th century. Leading the way was the "supply-side" philosophy of outsourcing jobs, under the guise of free trade. Outsourcing jobs is NOT trade. Without reasonable paying jobs, there cannot be enough sales, as China has found out. Another of those major mistakes was the failure to correct our money creation system of debt money. The current global monetary system is unsustainable and will eventually collapse the economy. Monetary reform, described in Section I, allows us to fund future programs to sustain a healthy capitalistic economy.

Many economists think that innovation and expansion will solve the issue, as it has done before, but they are thinking nationally, not globally. If we look globally, there are well over two billion unemployed and subsistence farmers. Our successful and productive capitalistic system does not need all these workers to make all of our goods and services. Mind you, these workers are working 40 plus hours a week. The age of scarcity is over! We can make and grow all the goods and services that everyone needs, but we do not have enough money to buy them! It is going to get worse. An example is the movement of 90% of the population needed in agriculture to grow our food in the 19th Century, to 2% in the 20th Century. The new technology of AI, Robotics, 3D Printing and Nanomanufacturing will start eliminating net jobs! The following will be a short discussion on each, followed by solutions:

Robots have been around for decades, but now there has been a major breakthrough. A company has built and has started to sell a robot called "Baxter". The two differentiating factors are price and the ability to work next to humans without hurting them. These are labeled collaborative robots or cobots. The cost of Baxter is only $22,000, which results in an hourly operating cost of $4 per hour including the price of purchase. Robots work 24/7, don't get sick, go on vacation, go on strike, and make no mistakes. As they are mass produced, they will get cheaper and better.

By the end of the century, most blue collar workers will be replaced. In fact, today, we have two new robotic systems replacing Mexican farm workers in the Imperial Valley. I believe that they will waterproof Baxter and he will do all the rice farming that subsistence farmers are doing now. There is also a low cost robotic system for our kitchens about to go to market that can do the cooking, developed by Mark Oleynik and recently displayed in a fair in Germany.

131

"Middle skilled jobs are the ones most affected by automation," said Adam Keiper, editor of The New Atlantis and a fellow at the Ethics and Public Policy Center in Washington. "In the service sectors – like restaurant wait staff, hotel personnel, and certain kinds of medical professionals. And 25 percent of the jobs that exist today won't exist in the next 20 to 30 years. To put it into context, that is about the unemployment rate of the Great Depression." Furthermore, because of robotics, Randy Bateman, an economist, expects dangerous jobs to be replaced, such, as those of soldiers, firefighters, police officers, loggers and fishermen. Dirty jobs, he said, also would be jettisoned, including agricultural types, waste disposal personnel and slaughterhouse workers.

In a recent *National Geographic* article, there was a picture of a caretaker robot assisting an elderly monk in Thailand. The *Economist* magazine just reported on a robotic sewing machine that can replace the low wage sweatshop, and garment workers. The scientists in Japan have programmed a robot to help an elderly person out of bed and into a wheelchair. They also have robots that check you into a hotel and a robot bellman to take your luggage to your room. Boston Dynamics has a new bipedal robot that performs human tasks. Not to mention the much publicized self-driving cars, this innovation will eventually replace taxi drivers. What about all those long haul truck drivers? It has already started. I envision convoys of self-driving trucks escorted by maintenance and security vehicles. These robotic advancements are life changing and job killing! Many predict this will be in full force within 10 to 30 years. Robots will also do the many future jobs that don't even exist today.

3D printers are starting to show up in many places in the business community, and currently they are finishing up the final stages of an inexpensive one for the home. Instead of ordering, making and delivering replacement parts to the retail store or human body parts to the consumer, one just has to go to your 3D printer, which retrieves the software from the cloud to create the part you want. All you need to do is put in the appropriate toner to build the part. You do need periodic repair and maintenance, but there are no workers necessary to build and deliver the new part. Body parts are still experimental, but getting close.

Nanomanufacturing is the newer of discoveries, which is basically building things one atom at a time by tiny nanomachines. These machines are self-replicating and programmable, so you can direct them to build anything you want.

Yes, these advancements, and others like AI (Artificial Intelligence), will provide for jobs for their manufacture and maintenance, but not nearly enough to replace the millions of jobs they will eliminate. We also continue to have innovations and increased service, but again, not nearly enough to adequately employ the global work force.

Around the world we have all this production with management continually attempting to reduce labor costs, but if nobody is working, how can they afford to buy anything? What should we do? Let's take the non-economic factor of people dedicated to their jobs of 30, 40, 50, 60 hours a week. Work is an important social and psychological factor in the human condition. What are they going to do with their time? How can all of them be retired or semi-retired? People will spend more time developing themselves. There will be more charity, travel, culture, entertainment, research & development, exploration, environmental clean-ups, physical and mental self-improvement efforts. These industries will boom! See "Wonderland – How Play Made the Modern World" by Steven Johnson.

The actual implementation of the following policies should be done **gradually** as the economic environment evolves to avoid excess inflation. The macroeconomic policies are basically the governments providing the money and benefits to create quality customers as their jobs are reduced and eliminated. No, we are not going to be all the same! This system will gradually provide the basic necessities of modern life. **There still will be the rich, but not the poor.** We will still have to work to get extras like bigger homes, flat screen TVs, cars, and vacations, etc. These recommendations are for the global economy.

1. Since the demand for labor will be reduced by technology, we should go the other route and share the amount of work available more evenly by gradually reducing the work week, eliminate 60+ hour work weeks in the third world, and start moving towards France's 35-hour work week
2. Gradually start increasing the guaranteed vacation time, paid sick leave, and paid family leave--moving towards France's six-week vacation policy. The U.S. does not even have any guaranteed vacation time!
3. Provide food stamps for all, using the current credit card system.
4. Free schooling from two years old through university.
5. Pay most of healthcare costs for all (including dental, physical and mental, including addictions and nursing homecare)
6. Provide a stipend for residential assistance. Take a look at the city of Berlin's solution to lack of residential supply, causing high prices. Berlin requires nonresidential building projects to build an equivalent of 20% of its project in residential construction. The residential building does not have to be in the same commercial building. Along with moderate rent control it provides a substantial supply of apartments that keep the rents low. This follows Section III, reducing the flaw of lack of competition
7. Provide a stipend for miscellaneous purchases, like transportation and clothing*
8. Reduce early retirement penalties on qualified plans like IRAs, pensions, 401ks, TSA's etc.

*This is similar to the universal basic income, national dividend or income concept. You can read Al Sheahen's *Basic Income Guaranteed: Your Right to Economic Security (Exploring the Basic Income Guarantee) (1983),* there is also a 2012 version. This is also the same concept of helicopter money developed by Milton Friedman, the father of monetarism. Note the State of Alaska provides an annual dividend to its citizens from its oil revenues. This basic income would be taxable.

Austria, Britain, Canada, Denmark, Finland, Germany, Ireland, Luxembourg, Norway and Sweden already have an allowance for children as high as $4,900 a year. Brazil and Indonesia have used cash payments to reduce extreme poverty and the latter used it to reduce the effects of extreme fundamentalists.

** The word "free" also means there could be a very small stipend. There can be some disadvantages to operationally provide completely free services because of potential overuse.

Yes, there will be goof-offs. Who cares! If they want anything extra, they will have to do some additional work. And if they want the real good life, they must have successful careers as they do now.

NO, this is not Socialism! It is <u>Consumerism!</u> All these goods and services will be provided, as they are now, mostly by private enterprise in a competitive marketplace with less wage pressures on business. The government's primary role will be to provide the money to purchase the goods and services. A country can start by first covering their citizens only, then their legal residents. Governments have to be careful to avoid overtasking system from illegal immigrants. To protect our consumers worldwide, we will still need quality customer minimum wages and hours, wage differential tariffs, labor unions, and more employment contracts. This will provide for a substantial increase in quality customers, clients, consumers, and citizens and creating a 21st Century Win-Win Economy. Remember, paying for basic living expenses substantially reduces or eliminates the need for many social programs, such as: welfare and unemployment programs, social security disability and Medicaid. At the same time, it reduces crime caused by providing basic expenses for survival.

Chapter 34

CARE & PROTECTION OF

CUSTOMERS/ CLIENTS/ CONSUMERS/ CITIZENS

To have a quality economy, the most important thing is not how much people have on the top, but how much people have at the bottom in order to be quality customers/clients/consumers/citizens (c/c/c/c).

In this age of non-scarcity, a quality c/c/c/c is a healthy person or family that has the minimum necessities of life, funded by a federal government that allows them to work for extra funds to purchase additional desired goods and services and save extra for retirement.

Can you image how many great customers businesses could have by eliminating most health insurance costs, basic food expenses, low or no educational expenses through college, and a residential subsidy?

By eliminating/reducing all federal income and payroll taxes on all families making $100,000 or less, they will be able to consume without much debt except for large items like homes and cars. This can be accomplished when more funding is provided by the monetary system (See Section I.) along with taxes, usage fees and adding a royalty income for the governments funding of higher risk research (see Mazzucato's "The Entrepreneurial State"). The reduction of federal taxation will also allow for more individual state taxation to fund their selected programs.

It is up to businesses (owners and capitalists) and government to establish policies for the care and protection of their c/c/c/c, which includes their employees. **It is in their own self-interest!** Implementation and ownership will still be in mainly private hands, avoiding a socialistic state.

Chapter 35

SUMMARY OF SOLUTIONS

Section I – "Not Enough Money"

1. Eliminate the money creation powers of the Commercial Banks and The Federal Reserve. Empower the legislative branch or a new monetary authority with the power of money creation; operating with many checks and balances. Monetary reform will take Congressional legislation for implementation

2. Distribute this new money through three vehicles: debt, equity and direct currency issue using at least 10 different distribution systems including government spending. This will create a substantial increase in the quality of customers/consumers/clients. This will complete the funding of the conversion from fossil fuels, environmental cleanup and infrastructure repair

3. Initiate all the "excess **inflationary** protocols"

4. Pay off all Treasuries as they mature with zero coupon bonds or just money (We could also pay off all student loans or lower interest to 1% or less.)

5. Move the Federal Reserve into the Treasury Department as a bank regulator, keeping a form of FDIC deposit insurance, for the savers and the banks, creating a Win-Win scenario

Section II – "Not Enough Customers"

Short Term

1. Attempt to minimize competition on the basic cost of living by installing a quality customer minimum wage

2. Introduce wage differential tariffs against low wage countries to encourage significant increases in offshore consumers and to protect our own

3. Encourage more labor union development with proper oversight

4. Establish standard universal employment contracts

Long Term – preparing for a Robotic Age

1. Gradually provide more basic life services and/or just money to counter the decline of jobs including food, health, education, transportation and shelter.

2. Start decreasing working hours and increasing vacation time.

3. Increase the ability to retire early.

Section III – "Not Enough Competition"

1. Increase the number of researchers, economists and attorneys in the Antitrust Division of the Justice Department

2. Increase the breakup of monopolies and oligopolies

3. Increase the scrutiny and reduce the number of mergers and acquisitions

4. Change the name of this division to the Competitive Division

5. Encourage and develop a global effort in this arena

6. Establish, a utility like "Monopoly Commission" to control pricing and deceptive practices on monopolies and some oligopolies. This operation can be local and/or federal

Section IV – "Lack of Long-Range Planning"

1. Make dividends tax deductible to the C Corporation

2. Alter CEO and other executives pay to encourage more long range planning

3. Stock repurchase programs should be controlled and restricted

4. Reduce the power of control the executives have over the Board of Directors

5. All community leaders, both elected and nonelected need to encourage more long range planning

6. Encourage more corporate social responsibility programs

Section V – "Other Economic Topics"

1. Taxes – After implementation of monetary reform lower payroll and income taxes on everyone making less than $100,000. Separate the capital gains tax and make it more progressive. Lower the corporate net income tax and start a corporate gross profits tax. Keep the Estate Tax and make it more progressive

2. Health Care – Introduce a Medicare Productivity Act (lowering costs) with increased fraud investigations. Open Medicare to all with insurance companies providing the administration and supplemental policies. Expand the National Health Service for emergencies and providing rural health care

3. Environment – Implement environmental differentiation tariffs to increase sustainable environmental practices in those countries that are sufficiently behind the U.S's practices. Insure the

implementation of the 5 R's: Recycle, Reuse, Regenerate, Repair, and Renewables

4. Regulations – Reduce over regulating the good and increase looking for the bad

5. Ownership – Increase the ownership of businesses to more people

6. Education – Free education for all and require one semester of a financial planning course in high school

7. Usury – install a maximum one can charge for a loan

8. Corporate Governance – Increase the control of the actual owners over management

9. Make Social Security more macro economically favorable by taxing the higher income earners more and paying out a closer to parity amount

The previous outlines are the specific steps for creating a Win-Win Economy by creating proper recirculation and new money diversity. All business sectors will flourish while providing quality living conditions for all. Even commercial and investment banking will prosper. Some parts of the commercial banking sector will have to make adjustments but there will be a substantial amount of new operations. The investment bankers will not have a significant profit center in buying and selling government securities but they will have a significant amount of newly created low inflationary money and they will prosper.

It will take a significant effort for our political leaders to research the alternatives and their details in order to pass legislation. Let's vote for the leaders that are willing to move out of the box, **start the debate** and work. "If we cannot change economic policy through elections, then elections are irrelevant and it is useless to vote." This is a quote by George Kitrongalos, the administrative reform minister in the new Synisa government in Greece.

The majority of voters around the world vote their pocket book. Their leaders at that time get the praise or the blame for the condition of the economy. But the politicians are not in charge. The actual economy depends on how much money is in diverse circulation for spending and investing. We need to put our leaders in charge of the main source of the money creation process. Voters think they are now. If they do a bad job, as the commercial banking system has done, we then can vote them out!

Glossary of Terms:

Aggregate Demand: The sum of all demand within an economy, making up national income and expenditure.

(Aggregate) Supply: The total of all goods and services produced in an economy, less exports, plus imports.

Annual deficit: An excess of expenditures over revenues (mostly taxes) received. This amount is borrowed and added to the national debt.

Anti-Trust: Legislation to control monopoly and restrictive practices that hinder competition.

Bankruptcy: A declaration by a court of law that an individual or company is insolvent, that is, cannot meet its debts on the due dates.

Bond: A form of loan (security) issued by central or local governments, companies, banks or other institutions. Bonds are usually a form of long-term debt (security or loan).

Bretton Woods: An International Conference was held at Bretton Woods, New Hampshire, U.S.A. in July 1944 to discuss alternative proposals relating to post-war international payment problems put forward by U.S., Canadian and U.K. governments.

Budget: An estimate of income and expenditures for a future period as opposed to actual receipts and expenditures.

Capacity: The maximum amount of goods and services that could be produced by a whole economy.

Capital gains: A realized increase in the value of capital asset, as when a share or stock or real estate is sold for more than the price at which it was purchased.

Capital market: The market for longer-term loanable funds as distinct from the short-term funds. The capital market is an international one and is not one institution in any one country.

Capitalism: A social economic system in which individuals are free to own the means of production and maximize profits and in which resource allocation is determined by the price system.

Central bank: The instrument of the government's function to control the credit system and the power to create new money. A bankers' bank and lender of last resort. Federal Reserve is the central bank of the United States.

Commercial banks: Privately owned banks but regulated by government. Their major function is receiving deposits (savings accounts) and making loans to individuals, companies and other organizations.

Consumer Price Index (CPI): An index of prices of a specified basket of goods and services purchased by consumers to measure the rate of inflation or the cost of living.

Debt: A sum of money or other property owned by one person or organization to another. Debt requires debt servicing which consists of paying interest on the owed amount.

Deflation: Persistent decrease in the general level of prices.

Depression: An imprecise term given to a severe and prolonged economic downturn more severe than recession with a sustained high-level of unemployment.

Developing country: A country that has not yet reached the stage of economic development characterized by neither the growth of industrialization, nor the level of national income sufficient to yield the domestic savings required to finance the investment necessary for further growth.

Economic growth: The increase in a country's per capita national income. There are problems in the measurement of national income; as many activities may not take place in a market where statistics are collected.

Economics: The study of production, distribution and consumption of wealth to human society. There never has been a definition that is acceptable to all.

Equity-ownership: The values of an asset after all outside debt (liabilities) have been satisfied, such as equity in your home. Stock in the stock market is considered equity.

Exchange rates: The price (rate) at which one currency is exchanged for another currency.

Federal Reserve System: The central banking system of the United States established by the Federal Reserve Act of 1913 and modified by the Banking Act 1935.

Fiscal power or policy: The ability of any government to collect taxes and spend whatever collections the policy determines can be taxed and spent.

Gross Domestic Product (GDP): A measure of the total flow of goods and services produced by the economy over a specific period. It is obtained by valuing outputs of goods and services at market prices and their aggregating.

Gross National Product (GNP): Gross domestic product plus the income to domestic residents arising from investment abroad, less income earned in the domestic market occurring to foreigners abroad.

Inflation: Persistent increased in the general level of prices.

Infrastructure: Roads, airports, sewage and water systems, railways, the telephone and other public utilities.

Interest rate: The proportion of a sum of money that is paid over a specific period of time in payment for its loan. It is the price a borrower has to pay to use cash which he/she does not own and the return a lender enjoys for deferring his/her consumption or parting with liquidity.

International Monetary Fund (IMF): It was set up by the United Nations Monetary and Financial Conference at Bretton Woods in 1944. The fund was established to encourage international cooperation in the monetary field and the removal of foreign exchange restrictions, to stabilize exchange rates and to facilitate a multilateral payment system between countries.

Investment Bank or Merchant Bank: A financial intermediary (old money) which purchases new issues and places them in small parcels among investors. Although called a bank, they are not the same as commercial banks who have new money creation ability.

Keynes economics: The branch of macroeconomic theory and doctrines that tends to support the following:
1.) Aggregate demand plays a decreased role in determining the level of real output.
2.) Economics can settle at positions with high unemployment and exhibit no natural tenancy for unemployment to fall.
3.) Governments, primary through fiscal policy, can influence aggregate demand to cut unemployment.
Keynes, John Maynard (1883-1946): English economist whose major work was the General Theory of Employment, Interest and Money.

Laissez-Faire: The principle of the non-intervention of government in economic affairs that is supported by classical economists who adopted the theme from Adam Smith in
Wealth of Nations.

Loan: The borrowing of a sum of money by one person, company, government or other organization from another. Loans are debt and may be secured or unsecured, bearing interest or interest free, long-term or short-term, redeemable or unredeemable.

Macroeconomics: The study of whole economic systems aggregating over the functioning of individual economic units. Macroeconomics is the study of national economies and the determination of national income.

Monetarism: The branch or theory of macroeconomics that holds that increases in the money supply are a necessary and sufficient effect on aggregate demand. Another tenet is that any change in aggregate demand the government succeeds in bringing about will manifest itself in the end in higher prices and not higher output.

Monetary policy: A national government's policy with respect to the quantity of money in the economy.

Money supply: The stock of liquid assets in an economy that can freely be exchanged for goods or services. Money supply is a phrase that can describe anything from notes, bills, coin, cash, bank deposits, checks, money markets.

Monopoly: A market in which there is only one supplier.

National debt: The total outstanding borrowing of a central government (country).

Natural resources: Commodities or assets with some economic value that do not exist because of any effort of humanity, such as gold, silver, and oil.

New Money: The first use of created money whether for spending or investment.

Old Money: The second and successive use of newly created money by anyone other than the national government.

Oligopoly: Market situation in which a small number of selling forms and individuals control the market supply of a particular good or service and are therefore able to control the market place. An oligopoly can be perfect, where all firms produce an identical good or service (cement) or imperfect, where each firm's product has a different identify but is essential to the others (cigarettes). Because each firm in an oligopoly knows its share of the total market for the product or service it produces, and because any change in price or change in market share by one firm is reflected in the sales of the others, there tends to be a high degree of interdependence among firms; each firm must make its price and output decisions with regard to the responses of the other firms in the oligopoly, so that oligopoly prices, once established, are rigid. This encourages non-price competition, through advertising, packaging and service—a generally nonproductive form of resource allocation. Two examples of oligopoly in the United States are airlines serving the same routes, and tobacco companies. (Directly from the Barron's Financial Guide Dictionary of Finance and Investment Terms.)

Open market operations: The purchase or sale of government bonds by the central bank to influence the supply of money, and so influence rates and the value of credit.

Productivity: An economic measure of output per unit of input.

Quantitative Easing: Quantitative easing is an unconventional monetary policy in which a central bank purchases government securities or other securities from the market in order to lower interest rates and increase the money supply. Quantitative easing increases the money supply by flooding financial institutions with capital in an effort to promote increased lending approaching zero, and does not involve the printing of new banknote.
Recession: An imprecise term given to a sharp slowdown in the rate of economic growth or a modest decline in economic activity.

Recirculation: Recirculation is a synonym of redistribution which means money is taken from the wealthiest and given to the less wealthy by taxation, usually increasing commerce if not too excessive.

Regulation: The supervision and control of the economic activities of private enterprise by government in the interest of economic efficiency, fairness, health and safety.

Socialism: A social and economic system in which the means of production are collectively owned (government) and equality is given a high priority.

Supply-side economics: Concerns with the factors affecting the supply of goods and services in the economy.

Surplus: The amount of taxes and other revenue collected by governments over the amount of expenditures.

Tariff: A tax imposed on imported goods and services.

Usury: The act or practice of lending money at a rate of interest that is too high or against the law.

Velocity of Circulation: The speed with which the money in an economy circulates or the number times it is used for consumption of goods and services generating commerce, profits and taxes.

World Bank: The World Bank was set up by the Bretton Woods agreement in 1944. Its purpose was to encourage capital investment for the reconstruction and development of the member countries, either by channeling the necessary private funds or by making loans from its own resources.

MARK PASH grew up and worked in two separate family businesses, one in manufacturing and the other in retail stores. He went on to receive two business degrees, Bachelors and Masters, from UCLA and USC respectively. Then he served, as an officer in the business branch of the U.S. Army in the Quartermaster Corp. After the Army, he received his Certified Financial Planning designation from the College of Financial Planning and the Institute of Certified Financial Panners, now the CFP Standards Board.

Over the past 45 years Mark has been very active in the financial industry helping clients with their budgets, investments, loans, income taxes, social security, medical coverage and scores of other business and personal financial issues. He was listed by Money Magazine as one of the top financial planners in the nation.

Additionally, Mark has founded a number of financial organizations and has served as an officer of various industry corporations and associations. His extensive background brings a grounded understanding of the practical and theoretical in the field of macroeconomics. He has written many articles besides his first book "Economic theory of Relativity" and the website of the nonprofit, Center for Progressive Economics at www.cpe.us.com. Mark has long been active in politics serving on various campaigns advisory committees and running for Congress.

Mark has been married for almost 50 years to his wife Ruth with two daughters, Andrea and Kim, with two grandchildren, Rayne and Zealand and son-in-law Michael Bell.

12496

Made in the USA
San Bernardino, CA
22 February 2017